Beauty for Truth's Sake

Beauty for Truth's Sake

The Re-enchantment of Education

Stratford Caldecott

BrazosPress
a division of Baker Publishing Group
Grand Rapids, Michigan

Published by Brazos Press
a division of Baker Publishing Group
P.O. Box 6287, Grand Rapids, MI 49516-6287
www.brazospress.com

Printed in the United States of America

Library of Congress Cataloging-in-Publication Data

Caldecott, Stratford.
Beauty for truth's sake : on the re-enchantment of education / Stratford Caldecott.
p. cm.
Based in part on a series of discussions and seminars held at Arkwood, N.H.
Includes bibliographical references and index.
ISBN 978-1-58743-262-0 (pbk.)
1. Education—Philosophy—Congresses. 2. Education, Humanistic—Congresses. I. Title.
LB14.7.C34 2009
370.1—dc22 2009009353

The best ideal is the true
And other truth is none.
All glory be ascribèd to
The holy Three in One.

Gerard Manley
Hopkins, *Summa*

Contents

Acknowledgments

The origins of this book lie partly in a series of discussions and seminars on education conducted at Arkwood in New Hampshire some years ago by David L. Schindler, with Glenn W. Olsen. I want to thank everyone who participated in those groups. Some parts of this book are based on essays I have written elsewhere, but all have been extensively revised or adapted from their original sources. In chapter 3, the sequence on Sacred Number is adapted with permission from David Clayton's article, "Art of the Spheres" in *Second Spring* 8. In chapter 5, a version of the section on "Humane Architecture" also appeared in *Second Spring* 8 (2007). Parts of chapter 6 were given as a paper to a Washington Arts Group conference in May 2007, "Jumping Out of the Self-Referential Box." I am grateful to David Clayton for his encouragement in the development of the ideas in this book through numerous conversations in Oxford, as well as to Michael S. Schneider, Frederick Stocken, Christopher Blum, Michael Augros, and Cyrus and Ben Olsen for reading and constructively criticizing parts of the manuscript. My thanks to Michael S. Schneider for giving me permission to use the illustrations on pages 58, 69, 72, 92, and 116. Finally, I want to thank Dr. Jeffrey O. Nelson and the Thomas More College of Liberal Arts for supporting me during the writing of this book, and my editors Rodney Clapp and Lisa Ann Cockrel for their encouragement and counsel in the final stages.

Please note that from time to time additional material of interest to readers will be posted in the "Books" section of the author's Web site at *www.secondspring.co.uk*.

Introduction

"To Sing with the Universe"

In the modern world, thanks to the rise of modern science and the decline of religious cosmology, the arts and sciences have been separated and divorced. Faith and reason often appear to be opposed, and we have lost any clear sense of who we are and where we are going.

Most of us are prepared to let developments in science and technology dictate the shape of the future. We see our job as being merely to hang on tight, to survive, and maybe take whatever advantages are offered us along the way. But in the process, despite all the excitement of modern life, we begin to notice not only that we are damaging the earth and destroying our fellow creatures, but that we are becoming less than human ourselves. We are reduced to being consumers and producers, producing merely in order to consume. We have more and more *stuff*, but the world seems thinner and less substantial, and our own souls also. We have gained much, but we have lost our way in the shadows.

Education is our path to true humanity and wisdom. By this I do not mean simply what goes on in school and university—which all too often turns out to be a path in another direction entirely away from both humanity and reason. I mean the broader process that engages us all through life. To be alive is to be a learner. Much of the learning we do takes place at home, in the family, or after we leave both home and college and begin the struggle to survive in the wider world. Increasingly, in a society shaped by technology that is continually changing, we need to learn a new skill: *how to keep learning*. We must be flexible and adaptable enough to survive in any circumstances. Even more important than flexibility is a virtuous character and set of guiding principles that will enable us to keep track of goodness amid the moral and social chaos that surrounds us.

I believe it is possible to remain an active learner throughout life, and yet to maintain a moral compass in good working order. But vital though they are, adaptability and ethics are not enough by themselves. There is a structural flaw in our education that we need to overcome. It is related to a profound malaise in our civilization, which by progressive stages has slipped into a way of thinking and living that is dualistic in character. The divisions between arts and sciences, between faith and reason, between nature and grace, have a common root. In particular, our struggle to reconcile religious faith with modern science is symptomatic of a failure to understand the full scope of human reason and its true grandeur.

The classical "Liberal Arts" tradition of the West once offered a form of humane education that sought the integration of faith and reason, and that combined the arts and the sciences, before these things became separated, fragmented, and trivialized. We need to retrace our steps, to find the "wisdom we have lost in knowledge," the "knowledge we have lost in information" (T. S. Eliot). The wisdom I am referring to can be traced back *via* Boethius and Augustine to Plato and Socrates; but before Socrates there was Pythagoras, and the Pythagorean contribution is just as important in helping us understand what was lost. This book is an attempt to discover and enter creatively into that Pythagorean spirit which lies at the root of Western civilization.

For every great change, every rebirth or *renaissance* in human culture, has been triggered by the retrieval of something valuable out of the past, making new, creative developments possible. The Italian Renaissance, for example, was triggered by the fifteenth-century rediscovery of the Classical Greek civilization. Similarly today, we may legitimately hope that *ressourcement*, a "return to sources," and in particular to the pattern of humane learning as it was traditionally understood in the West, though expressed in new ways, will lead to a *renaissance*, the birth of a culture more appreciative of life and wisdom.

It is significant that when the Cardinals of the Catholic Church elected a pope in 2005, they chose a *ressourcement* thinker—one whose concern was to retrieve, proclaim, and defend elements of the Catholic tradition that had been neglected in recent years. But one of the elements that Benedict XVI was most concerned to retrieve was something of much wider than Catholic interest. Speaking for example at Regensburg in September 2006, following the lead of his predecessor John Paul II in the encyclical *Fides et Ratio* ("Faith and Reason"), Pope Benedict XVI has attacked in the name of the whole Christian tradition the modern misconception that faith is the enemy of reason. Faith, he says, cannot be opposed to reason if it is placed in the second Person of the Trinity, who is the Word, the *Logos*, in whom "the archetypes of the world's order are contained."

The phrase I have just quoted comes not from the speech at Regensburg but from a passage in his book *The Spirit of the Liturgy*. The Pope's vision is one in which human existence is fundamentally "liturgical." That is to say, our lives can be oriented toward God by prayer and action in such a way that the interior world of the human soul and the exterior world of the society and universe are brought into harmony. Thus liturgy—which we often consider a purely human business, something of relevance only to religious believers—is closely related to the mathematical ordering of time, space, and matter. I will quote the whole passage because it is so important. Pope Benedict writes:

> Among the Fathers, it was especially St. Augustine who tried to connect this characteristic view of the Christian liturgy with the worldview of Greco-Roman antiquity. In his early work "On Music" he is still completely dependent on the Pythagorean theory of music. According to Pythagoras, the cosmos was constructed mathematically, a great edifice of numbers. Modern physics, beginning with Kepler, Galileo

and Newton, has gone back to this vision and, through the mathematical interpretation of the universe, has made possible the technological use of its powers.

For the Pythagoreans, this mathematical order of the universe ("cosmos" means "order"!) was identical with the essence of beauty itself. Beauty comes from meaningful inner order. And for them this beauty was not only optical but also musical. Goethe alludes to this idea when he speaks of the singing contest of the fraternity of the spheres: the mathematical order of the planets and their revolutions contains a secret timbre, which is the primal form of music. The courses of the revolving planets are like melodies, the numerical order is the rhythm, and the concurrence of the individual courses is the harmony.

The music made by man must, according to this view, be taken from the inner music and order of the universe, be inserted into the "fraternal song" of the "fraternity of the spheres." The beauty of music depends on its conformity to the rhythmic and harmonic laws of the universe. The more that human music adapts itself to the musical laws of the universe, the more beautiful it will be.

St. Augustine first took up this theory and then deepened it. In the course of history, transplanting it into the worldview of faith was bound to bring with it a twofold personalization. Even the Pythagoreans did not interpret the mathematics of the universe in an entirely abstract way. In the view of the ancients, intelligent actions presupposed an intelligence that caused them. The intelligent, mathematical movements of the heavenly bodies were not explained, therefore, in a purely mechanical way; they could only be understood on the assumption that the heavenly bodies were animated, were themselves "intelligent."

For Christians, there was a spontaneous turn at this point from the stellar deities to the choirs of angels that surround God and illumine the universe. Perceiving the "music of the cosmos" thus becomes listening to the song of angels, and the reference to Isaiah chapter 6 ["Holy, holy, holy is the LORD of hosts; the whole earth is full of his glory," Isaiah 6:3] naturally suggests itself.

But a further step was taken with the help of the Trinitarian faith, faith in the Father, the Logos [the Son], and the Pneuma [Holy Spirit]. The mathematics of the universe does not exist by itself, nor, as people now came to see, can it be explained by stellar deities. It has a deeper foundation: the mind of the Creator. It comes from the Logos, in whom, so to speak, the archetypes of the world's order are contained. The Logos, through the Spirit, fashions the material world according

> to these archetypes. In virtue of his work in creation, the Logos is, therefore, called the "art of God" (ars = techne!). The Logos himself is the great artist, in whom all works of art—the beauty of the universe—have their origin.
>
> To sing with the universe means, then, to follow the track of the Logos and to come close to him. All true human art is an assimilation to *the* artist, to Christ, to the mind of the Creator. The idea of the music of the cosmos, of singing with angels, leads back again to the relation of art to logos, but now it is broadened and deepened in the context of the cosmos. Yes, it is the cosmic context that gives art in the liturgy both its measure and its scope. A merely subjective "creativity" is no match for the vast compass of the cosmos and for the message of beauty. When a man conforms to the measure of the universe, his freedom is not diminished but expanded to a new horizon.[1]

The big themes in this passage are liturgy, mathematics, art, music, science, and worship. How are they all related? Through the "Logos," the Pope says. The Logos—meaning "Word," "Speech," "Principle," "Thought," and "Design," and identified by the fourth Gospel with Jesus of Nazareth—is the Mediator between heaven and earth, between the invisible One and the visible Many.

Western civilization has long since lost its sense that cosmic order has to be rooted in a "Logos." It is no coincidence that it lost its faith in God at the same time. If God is not connected with the universe by some kind of mediation, then he floats off into abstract space and faith starts to seem meaningless. Scientists, especially, have no use for such a God, and rightly so. Angelo Scola, the Patriarch of Venice who is another leading *ressourcement* theologian, has formulated the problem as follows:

> The question of meaning which Comte forbade us to ask re-surfaces inexorably, like those little clumps of grass that push through in the spring, even in the most desolate wastes. There is no point in avoiding the question of the primordial relationship between God and the

1. Ratzinger 2000, 152–54. Some paragraph breaks have been introduced for ease of reading. See also Chapp 2006, for a profound reading of this direction of the Pope's thought.

> human person, but we do need to formulate it in realistic terms. This involves the re-thinking of the mutual interrelationship between the world and the human person, *so as to recover the lost wisdom of the world*. Cosmocentrism and anthropocentrism can no longer go their separate ways, still less can they be posed as alternatives, if we want to do justice in our thinking to the original relationship between God and the human person.[2]

As we search for this "lost wisdom of the world," we will keep coming back to a rather significant fact. As our own eyes reveal every day, the universe is *beautiful*. It has majesty, order, and loveliness;[3] these three types of beauty are precisely what scientists themselves love to discover in the world. In fact the greatest of them have usually been motivated less by curiosity than by love. Plato would not have hesitated to call the longing for truth that drives them onward to their discoveries a form of erotic desire.[4]

And so, the chapters that follow are not just about education, although if taken seriously they would change the way we teach. They are also about the search for beauty in art, science, and the cosmos—in short, the search for the Logos. This search is partly a matter of retrieval, but again, not exclusively so. We must have a proper sensitivity to the positive insights and fruits of the Enlightenment, lest we reject the good along with the bad. Ancient writers too were often misled, and their ideas justly criticized and set aside. Let us apply the words of St. Basil the Great, writing about the Christian use of pagan literature in the fourth century, to the way we draw both from medieval and from modern writers whatever we may need to nourish our souls on wisdom today:

> It is, therefore, in accordance with the whole similitude of the bees, that we should participate in the pagan literature. For these neither approach all flowers equally, nor in truth do they attempt to carry off

2. Scola 2007 (my emphasis).

3. Corresponding to Father, Son, and Holy Spirit. I owe this suggestive distinction to Tom McCormick.

4. Science is a desire-driven quest—the question is, a desire for what? At its best, it is a desire for reality, attracted by the beauty of truth; at worst, simply for power over nature.

> entire those upon which they alight, but taking only so much of them as is suitable for their work, they suffer the rest to go untouched. We ourselves too, if we are wise, having appropriated from this literature what is suitable to us and akin to the truth, will pass over the remainder. And just as in plucking the blooms from a rose-bed we avoid the thorns, so also in garnering from such writings whatever is useful, let us guard ourselves against what is harmful.[5]

The following points may serve to sum up the thrust of the book.

- The way we educate is the way we pass on or transform our culture. It carries within it a message about our values, priorities, and the way we structure the world. The fragmentation of education into disciplines teaches us that the world is made of bits we can use and consume as we choose. This fragmentation is a denial of ultimate meaning. Contemporary education therefore tends to the *elimination of meaning*—except in the sense of a meaning that we impose by force upon the world.
- The keys to meaning are (and always have been) form, *gestalt*, beauty, interiority, relationship, radiance, and purpose. An education for meaning would therefore begin with an education in the perception of form. The "re-enchantment" of education would open our eyes to the meaning and beauty of the cosmos.
- Education begins in the family and ends in the Trinity. Praise (of beauty), service (of goodness), and contemplation (of truth) are essential to the full expression of our humanity. The cosmos is liturgical by its very nature.

This book can be no more than an initiation, an introduction to a certain view summarized in these three points. For those who wish to go further and deeper, I have tried to indicate in my notes and references resources that will assist. (I particularly recommend Michael S. Schneider's enormously rich and enjoyable textbook, *A Beginner's Guide to Constructing the Universe*.) But given the present crisis in education, and the desperate need to rethink the way we approach our

5. Basil the Great, from a sermon "To Young Men" cited in Gamble 2007, 184–85.

whole scheme of human knowledge, I make no apology for offering a kind of "manifesto," which inevitably skims over many important debates. It will be helpful to those who have recognized the problem, since it points in the only direction a solution may be found. To those who are confused about the purposes of education—including perhaps their own—it may throw some light into the shadows of our time. We do not need to be content with our fragmented worldview, our fractured mentality. It is not too late to seek the One who is "before all things" and in whom "all things hold together" (Col. 1:17). To all those who are on that journey this book is respectfully dedicated.

1

The Tradition of the Four Ways

[Socrates:] I am amused, I said, at your fear of the world, which makes you guard against the appearance of insisting upon useless studies; and I quite admit the difficulty of believing that in every man there is an eye of the soul which, when by other pursuits lost and dimmed, is by these purified and re-illumined; and is more precious by far than ten thousand bodily eyes, for by it alone is truth seen.

Plato, *The Republic*, Book 7[1]

Teachers often tell us that modern students don't know how to *think*. Setting aside the fact that this is a perennial complaint, made by teachers about their students in every age, it may be true that the conditions of modern life militate against independent thought in particular ways. Silence is rare, entertainment is all-pervasive, the pressure to consume-and-discard is almost irresistible. No one has put it better than G. K. Chesterton did in 1930: "People are inundated, blinded, deafened, and mentally paralysed by a flood

1. Plato 1892, 3:230.

of vulgar and tasteless externals, leaving them no time for leisure, thought, or creation from within themselves."[2] The situation has grown worse in every decade since.

No wonder students come to a college education expecting nothing more than a set of paper qualifications that will enable them to earn a decent salary. The idea that they might be there to grow as human beings, to be inducted into an ancient culture, to become somehow *more* than they are already, is alien to them. They expect instant answers, but they have no deep questions. The great questions have not yet been woken in them. The process of education requires us to become open, receptive, curious, and humble in the face of what we do not know. The world is a fabric woven of mysteries, and a mystery is a provocation to our humanity that cannot be dissolved by googling a few more bits of information.

The Great Tradition

The Liberal Arts tradition stands at the origin of the idea of university education in the West. The Liberal Arts (from *liber* meaning free) were intended to train man[3] in the use of his freedom, and to prepare the student for the higher study of philosophy and theology, through which one may become truly free, fully human.[4] (They were contrasted with the so-called "Servile Arts," which is not a term of contempt but covers branches of knowledge oriented toward practical ends or economic purposes, such as fabric-making, metalworking and architecture, commerce and agriculture, hunting, navigation, medicine, and entertainment.) In other words, philosophy and theology were not—as they have become—"subjects" defined by a certain content, on the same level as everything else, accessible

2. In a lecture at the University of Toronto called "Culture and the Coming Peril," paraphrased in Ward 1949, 500.

3. The concept of universal education, of course, is a modern one. Higher education traditionally excluded women, slaves, and indeed everyone except the free man or citizen whose calling was to rule and to contemplate. My intention in this book, however, is to use the word "man" inclusively as applying to both sexes.

4. See Pieper 1998, 21–26, and the longer account in Dawson 1989. For a broad selection of classic texts on education from Plato onward, see Gamble 2007.

to anyone. We had to *become capable of them*, and the Liberal Arts were our preparation. In the modern university this preparation is usually missing, and so are the higher studies themselves. Only the names are left.

University education is usually traced back to the Greek philosopher Socrates and his (moral) victory over his state executioners. In his own life he demonstrated his own teaching, summarized in the *Phaedo*, that philosophy is a preparation for dying; or rather, for dying *well*. Of course, Socrates, who wrote nothing down except in the immortal souls of his disciples, would have been unknown to later generations except for the work of one of those disciples, Plato. Through Plato's Academy from 387 BC and Aristotle's Lyceum from 335 until their closure possibly in AD 529, and the writings and followers of both men, the principles instilled by Socrates were transmitted and applied by later educators.[5]

What were those principles? In essence, that it is the nature and calling of the human being to *know*: to know truth, being, wisdom, goodness, virtue—the forms, or the highest causes. It is in knowledge that we transcend our limitations (including the limitations of mortality) and become identified with the truth that is our highest and deepest ground, beyond all that the senses can offer. But knowledge can only be attained through the systematic ordering of the soul or personality in pursuit of integrity; that is, the discipline of thought (by logic) and will (by virtue).

In Books 6 and 7 of his dialogue *The Republic*, Plato spends some time discussing the levels of being and the levels of knowledge, and the ascent of the mind through education. There are four levels of knowledge, the highest of which he calls reason (*nous*), followed by

5. The teaching of Socrates was imparted by a method of gentle but relentless questioning (*elenchus*). In this way he encouraged reasoned reflection about matters that the young men of Athens had previously been content to leave in the domain of mythology, awakening in them a desire not merely to "know" but to "understand." The figure of Socrates is the paradigm of the philosopher-sage. According to Pierre Hadot, ancient philosophy in general is misunderstood if we forget that the words on the page were merely a part, and not necessarily the most important part, of a series of spiritual exercises (Hadot 1995). As for the significant differences between Plato and Aristotle, whose influences on later tradition are intertwined, they cannot be examined here.

understanding, opinion, and the "perception of shadows" or mere sensory awareness. The power of learning exists in the soul, but "the instrument of knowledge can only *by the movement of the whole soul* be turned from the world of becoming to that of being, and learn by degrees to endure the sight of being, and of the brightest and best of being, or in other words, of the good."[6]

He then explores how the soul is to be moved as a "whole," in order to become acquainted with the highest reality, the "good." The key disciplines he proposes are arithmetic, plane and solid geometry, astronomy, and the study of harmony. In each case he distinguishes a lower and a higher use of the discipline, the lower being its employment for practical and worldly purposes and the higher for the purpose of finding "the beautiful and the good"—seeing through the patterns of the numbers or the stars to the eternal realities they can reveal to the inner eye of the mind. And when these different studies are pursued in this way, they converge and commingle:

> Now, when all these studies reach the point of intercommunion and connection with one another, and come to be considered in their natural affinities, then, I think, but not till then, will the pursuit of them have a value for our objects; otherwise there is no profit in them.[7]

It is then that they are severally taken up into what Plato calls the "hymn of dialectic," or philosophy, attaining "a conception of the essence of each thing" and a vision of the eternal light.

The "circle of learning" (from which we get our word *encyclopedia*) was systematized into nine fields of study by the Roman Marcus Varro in the first century after Christ, and refined by Augustine, Boethius,[8] and Cassiodorus into a list of seven divided into two groups. The first group, the *trivium* (three ways), consisted of:

- grammar
- rhetoric
- dialectic

6. Plato 1892, 3:218.
7. Ibid., 234.
8. For details see Chadwick 1981, 69–173.

These three *artes sermocinales* ("language studies"), taught through the study of literature, would enable a student to express himself, to communicate with others, and to argue effectively for a point of view. The second group comprised the *quadrivium* (or the four ways) of sacred sciences known as the *artes reales*, or *physicae*. These were the disciplines by which Plato believed the inner vision of the soul could be awakened:

- arithmetic
- geometry
- astronomy
- music

In fact they went back further than Plato, for it was the Pythagoreans who had originally grouped them together.[9]

Dorothy Sayers, in a well-known essay "The Lost Tools of Learning," provides an eloquent argument for the importance of reviving the *trivium* for young people today. Without a basic training in how to think, argue, and communicate, children are not ready for the study of "subjects" or equipped for the real world. We flood their environment with words, but they "do not know what the words mean; they do not know how to ward them off or blunt their edge or fling them back; they are a prey to words in their emotions instead of being masters of them in their intellects."[10] But Sayers's essay neglects the *quadrivium*, almost as though liberal education were a matter of the *trivium* alone. She implies that the former amounted to little more than a collection of topics, and reduces mathematics entirely to a branch of logic (for her it is "neither more nor less than the rule of the syllogism in its particular application to number and measurement").[11]

On the contrary, the *quadrivium* is essential to a liberal education in the traditional sense. And since we can normally only advance from sense-perception to intellectual intuition by way of intellec-

9. Kahn 2001, 13.
10. Sayers 1973, 118.
11. Ibid., 127.

tual argumentation, the *quadrivium* necessarily involved the study of number and its relationship to physical space or time, preparatory to the study of philosophy (in the higher sense of that word) and theology: arithmetic being pure number, geometry number in space, music number in time, and astronomy number in both space and time.[12]

Once generally accepted, the list of seven literate and numerate arts created a framework within which civilized thought and behavior could be transmitted down the generations. Classical educational ideals and literacy were preserved through the dark ages after the fall of Roman civilization within oases provided by the Benedictine and other monasteries. In the early ninth century, the Emperor Charlemagne, having reunited much of Western Europe by military conquest, tried to instill in his courtiers a love of learning with the help of monks he co-opted for the purpose (the foremost being Alcuin of York, known as the "schoolmaster of Europe"). In England, King Alfred did something similar later in the same century.

By the twelfth century, Hugh of St. Victor (d. 1141) was able to write in his *Didascalicon*:

> Out of all the sciences . . . the ancients, in their studies, especially selected seven to be mastered by those who were to be educated. These seven they considered so to excel all the rest in usefulness that anyone who had been thoroughly schooled in them might afterward come to knowledge of the others by his own inquiry and effort rather than by listening to a teacher. For these, one might say, constitute the best instruments, the best rudiments, by which the way is prepared for the mind's complete knowledge of philosophic truth. Therefore they are called by the name tri*vium* and quadri*vium*, because by them, as by certain *ways* (*viae*), a quick mind enters into the secret places of wisdom.[13]

Note the higher sense of "usefulness" operating in this text. Hugh is speaking of a higher-order utility than that of the Servile Arts, since

12. Thus John Henry Newman in *The Idea of a University* speaks of a liberal education as consisting of four studies—Grammar, Rhetoric, Logic, and Mathematics. The fourth contains the entire *quadrivium*: Geometry, Arithmetic, Astronomy, and Music (Newman 1982, 195).

13. Hugh of St. Victor 1991, 86–87.

it involves the acquisition of skills that liberate the learner from further dependence on a teacher, and conduce by stages to philosophic wisdom, and meditation on what is revealed by holy scripture, as the highest end of man.

Within this general framework, and from the schools associated with great cathedrals, there developed by the thirteenth century communities of scholars bound together by formal charter—the first "universities" in the West: Bologna, Paris, and Oxford. A Master of Arts degree was succeeded (for those who could persevere for up to twelve more years of education) by a Doctorate in higher studies. The earliest such university, that of Bologna, began as a faculty of law, Paris came to specialize in theology, while Oxford developed a concentration on mathematics and natural science.

Faculty of
THEOLOGY or DIVINITY

Faculty of
LAW

Faculty of
MEDICINE

Faculty of
ARTS or PHILOSOPHY
Trivium (B.A.) followed by *quadrivium* (M.A.)
then Philosophy (metaphysical, natural, and moral)

The four Faculties in a medieval university c. 1400

In the East a variety of institutions devoted to intellectual study had already emerged as successors to the great center of learning at Alexandria conquered by the Muslims in 642, both in Byzantium, where the Palace School functioned essentially for a thousand years from 425, and within the Islamic world, most famously Baghdad's "House of Wisdom" founded in 813 by a caliph allegedly inspired to do so by Aristotle in a dream. These had accumulated a great treasure of texts from the classical world (Euclid, Aristotle, etc.) and commentaries upon them. The relatively easy flow of this information around and into Europe between and among Christian, Jewish, and Islamic scholars (especially in Salerno and Toledo) was a distinctive characteristic of the twelfth century and helped to lay the foundations of the modern world.

Arguably, despite the great achievements of medieval civilization, in general the potential of the Liberal Arts for intellectual and spiritual integration failed to be manifested. Scholastic disputation certainly refined the power of thought. It led Aquinas to the important distinction between philosophy and theology, and this contributed to the emergence of a distinct department of philosophy within the faculty of Arts—a process that began in the thirteenth century. Furthermore his recognition that God causes creatures to be subordinate but real causes in their own right made possible the emergence of the natural sciences. Pope Benedict XVI writes:

> It is the historical merit of Saint Thomas Aquinas—in the face of the rather different answer offered by the Fathers, owing to their historical context—to have highlighted the autonomy of philosophy, and with it the laws and the responsibility proper to reason, which enquires on the basis of its own dynamic . . . Thomas was writing at a privileged moment: for the first time, the philosophical works of Aristotle were accessible in their entirety; the Jewish and Arab philosophies were available as specific appropriations and continuations of Greek philosophy. Christianity, in a new dialogue with the reasoning of the interlocutors it was now encountering, was thus obliged to argue a case for its own reasonableness. The faculty of philosophy, which as a so-called "arts faculty" had until then been no more than a preparation for theology, now became a faculty in its own right, an autonomous partner of theology and the faith on which theology reflected.[14]

But the rise of nominalism among the Franciscans undermined a metaphysical vision of the cosmos,[15] and the over-specialization of university faculties led to a breakdown in the essential conversation between disciplines. Apart from a few great thinkers and teachers

14. Benedict XVI, Lecture at the University of Rome "La Sapienza," January 17, 2008. There is an interesting account of this process in MacIntyre 1990, 156–57.

15. I will touch on this again in chapter 5 (the section on architecture), chapter 6, and in the conclusion. The breakdown of the medieval worldview and the reasons for the decline of sacred science are summarized in Bouyer 1988 (chap. 12) and Nasr 1996 (chap. 4). Cf. Dupré 1993.

such as Aquinas and Bonaventure,[16] the medieval ideal was instantiated most perfectly not in the universities at all, but in the great cathedrals such as Chartres, Amiens, and Notre Dame—and in the liturgies they were designed to serve. Here the sacred sciences of the *quadrivium* were expressed in massed stone and statuary, rose windows and labyrinths, and in the interplay between light, music, and sacramental gesture.

Meanwhile technological progress made in the Servile Arts, also known as the Mechanical Arts, coupled with the new notion that the purpose of "science" was to be useful—which had come to mean obtaining power over nature rather than wisdom[17]—was to reshape the world in ways that the ancient and medieval authors could hardly have conceived.

Adapting the Medieval Model

It is fairly clear that if the Seven Liberal Arts model is to become an adequate basis for education today, whether in colleges or in less formal settings, it needs to be broadened and adapted. Even by the thirteenth century the Liberal Arts were bursting at the seams trying to incorporate new knowledge.

In *The Crisis of Western Education* and other works, Christopher Dawson argued that, while the universities should concentrate more on the Liberal Arts and less on the Servile Arts, a simple revival of the *quadrivium* would not be sufficient to bring about a return to right reason. Young people need to be made aware of the spiritual unity out of which the separate activities of our civilization have arisen, and his proposal was to do that by teaching culture *historically*, using the literature of medieval Europe rather than the classical sources the medievals themselves would have used. Teaching the story of Christian culture may be the best way to "maintain the tradition of liberal education against the growing pressure of scientific specialization and

16. See especially St. Bonaventure's lecture *De Reductione Artium ad Theologiam* (originally written around 1250), in some ways the most perfect medieval treatise on education.

17. Sir Francis Bacon formulated the now famous aphorism "knowledge is power" in 1597.

utilitarian vocationalism," he thought. (Thinking like this lay behind the development of the "great books" program in many American universities and colleges.)[18]

Symptoms of our educational crisis, such as the fragmentation of the disciplines, the separation of faith and reason, the reduction of quality to quantity, and the loss of a sense of ultimate purpose, are directly related to a lack of historical awareness on the part of students. An integrated curriculum must teach subjects, and it must teach the right subjects, but it should do so by incorporating each subject, even mathematics and the hard sciences, within the history of ideas, which is the history of our culture. Every subject has a history, a drama, and by imaginatively engaging with these stories we become part of the tradition.

We also need to confront the secular mind-set that makes the cosmological assumptions of the *quadrivium* almost unintelligible today (I will write more about this later). The sheer amount of information available in every discipline is far too great to be mastered by one person even in an entire lifetime. The purpose of an education is not merely to communicate information, let alone current scientific opinion, nor to train future workers and managers. It is to teach the ability to think, discriminate, speak, and write, and, along with this, the ability to perceive the inner, connecting principles, the intrinsic relations, the *logoi,* of creation, which the ancient Christian Pythagorean tradition (right through the medieval period) understood in terms of number and cosmic harmony.

In *The Idea of a University,* John Henry Newman, charged in the 1850s by the Archbishop of Armagh with the task of shaping a Catholic University for Ireland, defends the tradition of the Liberal Arts education and tries to adapt it to the needs of the modern world. The principle remains the same: knowledge is its own end—"worth possessing for what it is, and not merely for what it does."[19] It is not to be valued for the power it gives us over nature, or even for the moral improvement it may bring about in us (even if these things may flow from it). It is to be valued for its *beauty*. "There is a physical beauty

18. Dawson 1989, 145. Cf. Bloom 1987.
19. Newman 1982, 86.

and a moral: there is a beauty of person, there is a beauty of our moral being, which is natural virtue; and in like manner there is a beauty, there is a perfection, of the intellect."[20]

Newman writes that this perfection of the intellect consists in

> the clear, calm, accurate vision and comprehension of all things, as far as the finite mind can embrace them, each in its place, and with its own characteristics upon it. It is almost prophetic from its knowledge of history; it is almost heart-searching from its knowledge of human nature; it has almost supernatural charity from its freedom from littleness and prejudice; it has almost the repose of faith, because nothing can startle it; it has almost the beauty and harmony of heavenly contemplation, so intimate is it with the eternal order of things and the music of the spheres.[21]

Almost "supernatural," then, but not quite. ("Liberal Education," he writes, "makes not the Christian, not the Catholic, but the gentleman."[22]) Yet Newman, writing as he is about a Catholic university, insists that the supernatural must have its place, its entry point, in the circle of knowledge. After all, science, like poetry, begins with a search for unifying principles, and the unifying factor in creation is its relation to God. "I have said that all branches of knowledge are connected together, because the subject matter of knowledge is intimately united in itself as being the acts and work of the Creator."[23] That much could be said without a specific faith, yet as Newman argues, if revelation tells us something true about the Creator, that something has a bearing on all fields of study, and theology must be allowed a voice in the great conversation that is the modern university.

By Newman's time, of course, under the peculiar conditions of the Enlightenment, the earlier elevation of theological wisdom to the

20. Ibid., 92.

21. Ibid., 105. Newman is sometimes accused of being a nominalist, but a convincing case against this interpretation, based partly on his recognition of moral universals, is made by Merrigan 1991, 116–23.

22. Newman 1982, 91.

23. Ibid., 75. This was also the main point of Bonaventure's *De Reductione*, though the two approaches are very different.

position of being the end and goal of a liberal education had resulted in a separation of theology from the rest of the curriculum—even from philosophy, which could be said to have arisen as a separate subject precisely to mediate between theology and the *quadrivium*. In the new secular universities theology had the lower status of a specialization for professionals (those in training for the priesthood), or could be dismissed altogether. Newman had to fight an intellectual battle to defend the key role of theology in the complete university curriculum.

Theology, therefore, has an important place in the integration of the arts and sciences. Equally important, however, is a symbolic approach to number and shape—that is, the awareness that mathematics has a qualitative, as distinct from a purely quantitative, dimension. Mathematics is the language of science, but it is also the hidden structure behind art (the philosopher Leibnitz famously described music as the pleasure the human mind experiences from counting without being aware that it is counting), and its basis is the invisible Logos of God. We do not have to follow the ancient symbolic reading of mathematics slavishly, but only be open to the presence of meaning where the modern mind sees none. Then it may be that we will open up a lost dimension in which the disciplines themselves will discover their relationship to one another.

Pope Benedict XVI, in another address to university professors, called for a "new humanism" based on a broader concept of the human (one that respects our transcendent vocation) and a broader concept of reason itself.

> A correct understanding of the challenges posed by contemporary culture, and the formulation of meaningful responses to those challenges, must take a critical approach towards narrow and ultimately irrational attempts to limit the scope of reason. The concept of reason needs instead to be "broadened" in order to be able to explore and embrace those aspects of reality which go beyond the purely empirical. This will allow for a more fruitful, complementary approach to the relationship between faith and reason. The rise of the European universities was fostered by the conviction that faith and reason are meant to cooperate in the search for truth, each respecting the nature and legitimate autonomy of the other, yet working together harmo-

> niously and creatively to serve the fulfilment of the human person in truth and love.[24]

He went on to speak of the urgent need to "rediscover the unity of knowledge and to counter the tendency to fragmentation and lack of communicability" that afflicts the academic disciplines at present. (The fracturing of knowledge is of course also of concern to secularists such as Allan Bloom.) An education worthy of the name would develop an awareness of the totality through art and literature, music, mathematics, physics, biology, and history. Each subject has its own autonomy, but at its heart it connects with every other.

Beauty for Truth's Sake

If beauty is a key to that lost unity, it is because beauty (according to the medieval philosophers) is one of the "transcendental" properties of being, that is, properties found in absolutely everything that exists. These properties include being, truth, goodness, and unity. *Everything*, in other words, is true, good, and beautiful in some degree or in some respect. All that exists—because it gives itself, because it means something—is a kind of "light." It reveals its own nature and at the same time an aspect of that which gives rise to it. Beauty is the *radiance* of the true and the good, and it is what attracts us to both.[25]

Who will not admit that harmony is more beautiful than dissonance, health more beautiful than sickness, kindness more beautiful than cruelty? If you push the postmodern relativist, you will almost certainly be able to get an admission that he would prefer to look up at a gorgeous sunset than down into the latrine. Now why is that?

24. Benedict XVI 2007.

25. See the discussion in Reale 1997. Beauty is like light because it "makes us see the One in the proportional and numerical relations by which it unfolds in the physical dimension of the visible as well as at the level of the intelligible" (301). There have of course been many attempts to account for the experience of beauty in neurological terms. H. E. Huntley gives some examples in his book *The Divine Proportion*. But reductionist explanations have a fundamental weakness. Actual lived experience is irreducible. If consciousness can be correlated with events in the brain, the decision to give the one ontological priority over the other remains a philosophical decision.

Is it really just a matter of taste? The artist, architect, and designer Christopher Alexander once designed an empirical test to train people in their perception of beauty and of what he calls the quality of "life" in things.[26] In comparing any two objects chosen at random, Alexander shows how different types of questions determine the *level* of our response to the objects. For example:

1. Which is the more *attractive* of these two objects?
2. Which do you like best? *Why* do you like it?
3. Which gives you the most *wholesome* feeling?
4. Which of them better represents *your whole self*?
5. If you had a choice, which would you *spend eternity with*?
6. Which of them would you be happier to *offer to God*?

Questions 4, 5, and 6 evoke a deeper response, and he finds that ninety percent of his students end up selecting the same object when asked these questions, whereas they will rarely do so if asked the first three questions.

According to Socrates, "The object of education is to teach us to love what is beautiful."[27] He meant, of course, what is *objectively* beautiful. We have been taught that beauty is a matter of feeling. That is not entirely wrong. The perception of beauty has to do with feelings, but this does not mean it is "purely subjective." Feelings, if properly refined and educated, can help us tell the difference between true and false.[28]

It is not just the artist who needs to orient himself in a dimension of objective truth and beauty. The same applies to the scientist, as I have already suggested. Physicist David Bohm emphasizes the relevance of beauty to science:

> Now, there is a common notion that beauty is nothing more than a subjective response of man, based on the pleasure that he takes in seeing what appeals to his fancy. Nevertheless, there is much evidence that

26. Alexander 2004.

27. Cited in Taylor 1998, 17.

28. None of which is to deny the very real beauty to be found in modern and postmodern works. Beauty exists in many modes as well as degrees, and the definition of beauty is by no means as easy as the medieval scholastics thought.

> beauty is not an arbitrary response that happens to "tickle" us in a pleasing way. In science, for example, one sees and feels the beauty of a theory only if the latter is ordered, coherent, harmonious with all parts generated naturally from simple principles, and with these parts working together to form a unified total structure. But these properties are necessary not only for the beauty of a theory, but also for its truth.
>
> Of course, in a narrow sense, no theory is true unless it corresponds to the facts. But as we consider broader and broader kinds of theories, approaching those of cosmology, this notion becomes inadequate . . . In the broad sense with which cosmology is concerned, the universe as a whole is to be understood as "true to itself"—a unified totality developing coherently in accordance with its basic principles. And as man appreciates this, he senses that his own response with feelings of harmony, beauty, and totality is parallel to what he discoveries in the universe. So, in a very important way, the universe is seen to be less alien to man than earlier excessively mechanistic points of view seemed to indicate.[29]

Another quotation will emphasize why beauty is essential, and what happens when it is neglected. This is from Hans Urs von Balthasar, who has had the courage to rewrite the history of theology from the point of view of beauty in his seven-volume work *The Glory of the Lord*:

> We no longer dare to believe in beauty and we make of it a mere appearance in order the more easily to dispose of it. Our situation today shows that beauty demands for itself at least as much courage and decision as do truth and goodness, and she will not allow herself to be separated and banned from her two sisters without taking them along with herself in an act of mysterious vengeance.[30]

Elsewhere he describes what happens when the relationship that should exist between nature and grace is destroyed, and beauty is lost after all:

> Then the whole of worldly being falls under the dominion of "knowledge," and the springs and forces of love immanent in the world are overpowered and finally suffocated by science, technology and cy-

29. Bohm 1996, 39–40.
30. Balthasar 1982, 18.

> bernetics. The result is a world without women, without children, without reverence for love in poverty and humiliation—a world in which power and the profit-margin are the sole criteria, where the disinterested, the useless, the purposeless is despised, persecuted and in the end exterminated—a world in which art itself is forced to wear the mask and features of technique.[31]

Thus the person who sneers at beauty "can no longer pray and soon will no longer be able to love."[32] Prayer can only be motivated by a love that reveals the beauty we long for, denial of which cuts off at its root the ability to pray.

Beauty on the Cross

Both science and art operate and live in the depth-dimension of things, exploring aspects of beauty and truth.[33]

For Christians, the place to look for answers to all the important questions is the Cross of Christ. In that Cross, read in the light of faith and tradition, we can find the keys to unlock the doors of the world. And what we see there is not a distant world of Platonic archetypes, but the Archetype of archetypes wedded to the world, and allowing itself to be crushed by the world in order to transform it.

Perhaps a scientist would see on the Cross an answer to the question, *What is science?* For science is about the quest for knowledge, and here we have the image of knowledge, of ultimate realism about the world and the way it works. Jesus the Logos submits to that fallen world, he allows it to act upon him, in order to reveal its true nature. In a faint and feeble way, the scientific method finds its archetype here, albeit infinitely transcended.

We can also read there an answer to the question, *What is art?* And we see that art is not necessarily "beautiful" in any superficial way. The figure on the Cross, covered in blood and spittle, has been made

31. Balthasar 1968, 114–15.

32. Balthasar 1982, 18.

33. Goodness too, although I have not dwelt on the ethical dimension of science. Neither science nor art operate outside the moral sphere, and to emancipate them entirely from morality is just as bad a mistake as to emancipate them from beauty.

repulsive by torment. What we see, nevertheless, is the supreme work of art. We see a divine act that takes existing matter, the matter of history and prophecy, and weaves it into a new design, a fulfilment that could not have been expected or predicted but, seen by those who have the eyes and ears for it, is perfect, as though no stroke of the pen, no flick of paint, no note or chord, could be changed without diminishment. We see on the Cross an image that transforms the way we view the world. The passion of Christ the Logos changes the world and remakes it, creating something new of it, bringing life out of death.

On the further side of death, beyond the ugliness converted by an inward act into the supreme expression of love, in the body of the resurrected, even the wounds now shine like jewels. Beauty (as glory) exists in the Trinity before, during, and after time. David Bentley Hart writes:

> God's beauty is delight and the object of delight, the shared gaze of love that belongs to the persons of the Trinity; it is what God beholds, what the Father sees and rejoices in the Son, in the sweetness of the Spirit, what Son and Spirit find delightful in one another, because as Son and Spirit of the Father they share his knowledge and love as person. This cannot be emphasized enough: the Christian God, who is infinite, is also infinitely *formosus*, the supereminent fullness of all form, transcendently determinate, always possessed of his Logos. True beauty is not the idea of the beautiful, a static archetype in the "mind" of God, but is an infinite "music," drama, art, completed in—but never "bounded" by—the termless dynamism of the Trinity's life; God is boundless, and so is never a boundary; his music possesses the richness of every transition, interval, measure, variation—all dancing and delight. And because he is beautiful, being abounds with difference: shape, variety, manifold relation. Beauty is the distinction of the different, the otherness of the other, the true form of distance.[34]

It is, we should add, difference or otherness held in a unity that does not destroy uniqueness. As Hart explains, if the Trinity were instead a Duality, God would not be love but narcissism, and beauty would lose its radiance. It is the Holy Spirit, the fact that true love

34. Hart 2003, 177.

is always turned away from itself, pouring itself out for others, that makes it open and radiant, and creates room in the Trinity for the creation itself, as well as for all the suffering and all the sacrifice that creation involves. The Trinity is the home of the Logos and the shape of love. These are high secrets of our Western tradition, and together they offer the key to its renewal.

2

Educating the Poetic Imagination

> The whole world of images that surrounds us is a single field of significations. Every flower we see is an expression, every landscape has its significance, every human or animal face speaks its wordless language. It would be utterly futile to attempt a transposition of this language into concepts. Though we might try to circumscribe, even to describe, the content these things express, we would never succeed in rendering it adequately. This expressive language is addressed primarily, not to conceptual thought, but to the kind of intelligence that perceptively reads the *gestalt* of things.
>
> Hans Urs von Balthasar, *Theo-Logic*, vol. 1, 140

In the preceding sketch of the assumptions and history of the Four Ways, the educational *quadrivium*, I neglected an important element. For the Platonic and Aristotelian tradition, music was not just one of the subjects to be studied for a master's degree. In a certain broader sense the choral art was the foundation of the educational process. As we read in Plato's Laws, "The whole choral art is also in our view the whole of education; and of this art, rhythms and harmonies form the part which has to do with the voice."[1] Music in this wider sense included song, poetry, story, and dance ("gymnastic").

If Plato's dialogues appeared to be harsh on the poets, it was owing to a concern that poetry should be purified by a concern for the truth.

> Thus, a tradition of learning that began with Homeric epics as models of imitation in virtue and delight are now taken up for serious reflection and discourse under the genius of the West's first great philosopher. All of the educational experiences detailed in *The Republic* for the child—songs, poetry, music, gymnastic—are meant to awaken and refine a *sympathetic* knowledge of the reality of the True, Good, and Beautiful, by placing the child inside the experience of those transcendentals as they are contained in these arts and sensory experiences.[2]

Rhythm, harmony, and melody—the subject of formal study at a more mature stage of a child's growth—must from the earliest age penetrate deeply into mind and soul through imitation and natural enjoyment. Only in this way, by ordering the soul in harmony and giving it a sense of the meaning of proportion and relationship, can it be induced later to become fully rational, and to derive pleasure from the theoretic contemplation of ideas. The road to reason leads through the ordering of the soul, which implies the necessity of an education in love, in discernment, and in virtue.

"A Beauty Which Defies Time"

The same assumptions were made by Christian teachers. The greatest of these, perhaps, was St. Benedict, the founder of monasticism in the West. Cardinal Newman, himself a great teacher, associates the Poetic element with Benedict in the way he associates the Scientific with St. Dominic and the Practical with St. Ignatius, in what he calls the three eras of Christian education.[3] As the Roman Empire collapsed and the barbarians swept across Europe, the monasteries of St.

1. Plato 1892, 5:52, from bk. 2 of *The Laws*.
2. Taylor 1998, 15 (my emphasis).
3. Newman 2001.

Benedict formed a chain of sanctuaries, where civilization itself was preserved and reforged in the fires of liturgy. The monks were drawn by a stable form of life built on a wise monastic Rule, which itself was a supreme work of the poetic imagination. Their communities instantiated the ancient ideal of a "musical" education: an ordered life, proportionate, harmonious, disciplined, and (often) joyful. Body, soul, and spirit were catered for: manual work and prayer gradually transformed the landscape in the remote locations they chose to live. At the center of this way of life was the Mass, and the Breviary or "Divine Office" created as a way of praying the Psalms seven times a day (and once in the night). Time itself had been sanctified by the sevenfold spirit of Christ,[4] and the monk's soul could be tuned to the rhythm of the cosmos by entering into this spirit.

Beauty flows from beauty, and from these oases of the spirit flowed art in profusion: music, architecture, painting. Plainsong, developed from the ancient chants of Israel and then transformed by the advent of polyphony, gave the foundation for all that we now know as "Classical" music. The architecture of the great monasteries was devised in service of the harmonies of this music and the duties of prayer. The refined art of illumination grew from the great work of transcription, by which the great books of the past were handed down. In Northumbria the Benedictine movement met and absorbed the Celtic influence from the north and west, resulting in the gorgeous pages of the Lindisfarne Gospels—one of the few fragments of this civilization to survive a later period of iconoclasm. It was out of this milieu that Charlemagne and Alfred summoned the new schoolmasters of Europe.

In his classic study of monastic culture, Jean Leclercq writes of the monks' evident appreciation of symbolism and beauty. In the sense that they studied the classics for the enrichment of personality, they were humanists. It is apparent from their choice of texts to be

4. The Holy Spirit sent by Christ upon the Church is described in the book of Revelation as sevenfold (e.g., Rev. 3:1 and 4:5), and according to Church tradition based on Isaiah 11:2–3 the gifts of the Spirit are also seven. Since God makes the world in seven "days," it is only fitting for Christ's work of redemption and sanctification to repeat this fundamental structure in the New Covenant, which makes the world anew through the institution of the seven sacraments. Benedict echoes this pattern on the authority of Psalm 118[119]:164, referring to seven as a "sacred number" in ch. 16 of his *Rule*.

preserved, as well as the ones they wrote, that the reading of pagan literature and philosophy had helped them refine their human faculties. They lived intensely, as well as remotely, and as a result they drew civilization toward them.

> On the one hand, the liturgy developed their feeling for beauty; on the other, asceticism and the cloistered life forbade the pleasures of the senses either crude or refined. Consequently they delighted in beautiful language and beautiful poetry. Certainly they never kept any text which had not charmed them with its beauty. If they read and copied Ovid, for example, it is because his poetry is admirable. At times they drew moral lessons from these authors, but they were not, thanks be to God, reduced to looking to them for that. Their desire was for the joys of the spirit and they neglected none that these authors had to offer. So, if they transcribed classical texts it is simply because they loved them. They loved the authors of the past, not simply because they belonged to the past but because they were beautiful, with a beauty which defies time. Their culture has always been timeless—and it is for that reason that it was effectual.[5]

Another wise Benedictine, Denis Huerre OSB, the abbot president of the Subiaco Congregation during most of the 1980s, explores the intimate links between beauty and the process of *conversio* that is the heart of a monk's life. "Beauty is unable to bypass the senses," he writes, "(and this is the reason we can never afford to despise sensual delight), but the function of our senses is to enable beauty to penetrate within, to become that to which the heart of our mind can give assent." And he goes on to speak of the beginnings of this tradition:

> From the second century onward, beginning with Origen, an entire literature grew up devoted to the "spiritual senses," which is only a way to help us speak about how we are penetrated by beauty; about what it is to encounter beauty; about how it is that that which beauty engages must be the whole of what we are, the totality that comprises the senses, memory, and imagination, as well as spiritual insight; about how it is that through this action of beauty all these aspects of being

5. Leclercq 1978, 170–71.

> human are able to intercommunicate and integrate themselves into ordered harmony.[6]

With this spirit flowing through them, the monasteries shaped the poetic imagination of medieval civilization. The twelfth century renaissance was as much a product of the monastic as of the cathedral schools, and the high culture of the Christian humanist was rooted in the labor and contemplation of the monks over many centuries. As James S. Taylor points out, even Thomas Aquinas, though he later became a Dominican, was the product of a Benedictine upbringing, having been placed with the monks at Monte Cassino at an early age. The magnificent synthetic power of his intellect would have owed a great deal to his participation in the Latin chant of the *Scola cantorum*, the musical education that opened his consciousness to the harmonies of the spirit.

Rediscovering Poetic Knowledge

The "poetic" rationality of St. Thomas might appear primitive in the eyes of our more mechanistic age. But though we have gained a great deal in terms of power over nature—enough to begin to reshape the code of life itself—we seem to have lost the ability to understand what it is we control. The modern period has seen a concerted attack on our confidence in the *human capacity to know*. Deprived of a spiritual foundation, human reason churns away confidently for a few generations, but eventually it comes to a halt because it finds that the world has been ground to dust and ashes which clog up the machinery;

6. Huerre 1994, 88. There is a classic expression of the tradition in St. Bonaventure: "When the soul by faith believes in Christ as in the uncreated Word, who is the Word and the brightness of the Father, she recovers her spiritual hearing and sight, hearing to receive the words of Christ, and sight to view the splendours of that Light. When the soul longs with hope to receive the inspired Word, she recovers, because of her desire and affection, the spiritual sense of smell. When she embraces with love the Incarnate Word, inasmuch as she receives delight from him and passes over to him in ecstatic love, she recovers her sense of taste and touch. Having recovered the spiritual senses, the soul now sees, hears, smells, tastes and embraces her beloved, and can sing as a bride the *Canticle of Canticles*, which was composed for the exercise of contemplation" (Bonaventure 1956, 75).

it has been ground so small that nothing remains to give it savor or color, depth or inner life. For the truth that reason seeks is not within its own unaided reach. Small wonder, then, that the postmodernists, structuralists, and deconstructionists lose faith in the whole process, telling us that there are no facts, only interpretations, and that we should prefer strategy to truth, rhetoric to rationality.

The Romantic movement was a reaction against the early stages of this process, the "mysterious vengeance" of beauty, separated from goodness and truth by the assumptions of a narrower rationality. Romanticism sought spiritual light and meaning not through abstract thought but in the world of the imagination, through poetry, images, music, feeling, and story. Already in the older tradition that stems from Aristotle, cognition was thought to depend in part on the imagination, since all mental concepts were abstracted from sensory images or "phantasms." But empiricism and rationalism opened a gulf between self and object, man and cosmos. In their attempts to bridge it, many Romantics relied on feeling alone. That led to the solipsism and self-indulgence of late Victorian decadence. Some opened themselves to unconscious forces that proved hard or impossible to control. But Romanticism also points toward a more promising road, which we glimpse in the writings of J. W. von Goethe in Germany and his younger contemporary S. T. Coleridge in England.

Coleridge in a famous passage of his *Biographica Literaria* linked imagination with perception: "The primary Imagination I hold to be the living power and prime agent of all human perception, and as a repetition in the finite mind of the eternal act of creation in the infinite I AM."[7] The Oxford "Inklings"—C. S. Lewis, J. R. R. Tolkien, Owen Barfield, Charles Williams, and their friends—who stand partly in the tradition of Coleridge, certainly viewed imagination as a path to truth. Though they differed greatly in their philosophical and religious commitments, and in their styles of writing, they shared a common love of story and poesy without in any way denigrating intellect and reason. Lewis's discussion of truth in the epilogue to *The Discarded Image* carefully distinguishes between the types of knowledge embodied in different images and models—comparing

7. Coleridge 1983, 304.

those employed in the contemporary sciences, on the one hand, with those of the medieval *quadrivium*, on the other. Michael Ward has shown how deeply Lewis felt about the continuing importance of the "seven heavens" of ancient cosmology, the distinctive "characters" of the seven planets, which gave him the hidden structure of the Narnia Chronicles. The seven Chronicles were conceived not as mere entertainment but as an imaginative way of communicating truths. Symbolism and atmosphere can sometimes accomplish this more effectively than rational argument. *The Lion, the Witch and the Wardrobe*, for example, presents a "monarchical" (Jovian) picture of the world and human consciousness participating in the cosmic Logos. Within the context of such a world, the Christian Gospel makes much more sense. In the end, as Ward puts it, "Lewis's septet presents participatory deification, not of the planets in the divine nature, but of the children in the divine nature as it is understood by means of the planets."[8]

The philosopher Owen Barfield, beginning in 1928 with his book *Poetic Diction*, explored the common metaphysical roots of both language and consciousness. Possibly influenced by Barfield, Tolkien was a philologist who voyaged "inside language" where words and things converge, as though traveling back in time and consciousness to Eden itself, where Adam gave to things the names that corresponded to their real natures. From his schooldays he had been convinced he had, with others, a mission to transform our materialistic civilization by reintroducing it to the power of poetry, the power to reveal truth in the very act of creating.[9]

In modern times we have neglected the poetic or musical dimension that was presupposed in the Liberal Arts as originally practised, and infused into the Middle Ages by the Benedictines—the need to educate *the heart and the imagination*, not just to feel but to know.

8. Ward 2008, 237.

9. To Coleridge's primary and secondary Imagination Tolkien added the category "Art," the ability to give to a collection of images the inner consistency of reality, and its highest expression in "Fantasy," where we come closest to imitating God as the creator of worlds. For more on the imaginative grasp of truth particularly in Tolkien, see Caldecott 2005.

Can we learn something from the Christian Romantics that would help us recover this lost poetical dimension of the Liberal Arts?

James S. Taylor's *Poetic Knowledge: The Recovery of Education* is informed by the experience of the Integrated Humanities Program at the University of Kansas in the 1970s and '80s. In line with the best of the Romantic tradition, Taylor contrasts the mode of "poetic knowledge," an inward or intuitive grasp of the world, with the "scientific" mode of knowledge based on the gathering of mere facts. The former is emotional, sensory, empathetic, and involves the whole person in the act of knowing. Poetic intuition is knowledge by "connaturality" or participation, that finds *within the self* something that corresponds to the object, thus leaping over the barrier between self and other. So a person gazing at the stars, even if he cannot measure them in the way demanded by scientific knowledge, may be led to a part of himself in which those great distances and holy fires are felt to exist and possess a meaning.

"This transient motion of a beloved hand," writes Jacques Maritain, "it exists an instant, and will disappear forever, and only in the memory of angels will it be preserved, above time. Poetic intuition catches it in passing, in a faint attempt to immortalize it in time. But poetic intuition does not stop at this given existent; it goes beyond, and infinitely beyond." It grasps not merely "the singular existent which resounds in the subjectivity of the poet," but "all the other realities which echo in this existent, and which it conveys in the manner of a sign." Poetic intuition is perception by the "integrated powers of the soul."[10]

Taylor's eloquent defense of the poetic mode of knowledge claims for it an inherent superiority over science (and gives pride of place to music as formative of harmony in the soul). But it is not a question here of simply asserting the superiority of the arts. We need to acknowledge the immense value and power of the empirical method. At the same time we must show that empiricism itself need not be reductionistic in its methods or conclusions. C. S. Lewis writes in prophecy of a more holistic science:

> The regenerate science which I have in mind would not do even to minerals and vegetables what modern science threatens to do to man

10. Maritain 1954, 126, 131–41. See also 123n17.

himself. When it explained it would not explain away. When it spoke of the parts it would remember the whole. While studying the *It* it would not lose what Martin Buber calls the *Thou*-situation.[11]

We have bemoaned the compartmentalization that thrusts the two ways of looking at the world into separate boxes. But the greatest scientists have never ceased to be motivated by the desire to find beauty in their equations, and their breakthroughs are often the result of an intuition, or an imaginative leap. What I want to suggest is that the opposition between the "cultures" of science and the arts can be overcome by teaching science and mathematics themselves at least partly according to the poetic mode. In other words, the best way to teach them is by first awakening the poetic imagination. We need to reestablish—for the sake of science as much as for the arts—a truly humane education that, in Taylor's words, "begins with the senses, and the discovery and cultivation of harmony and beauty in the soul by way of the sense's natural affinity for the harmonious, proportionate, and the beautiful in nature and the arts."[12] If children were from an early age exposed to a "musical" training in the Greek sense, if their poetic sensibility was kindled by training in the observation of nature and the learning of poetry, and if mathematics and science were taught historically, with due attention to the symbolic and beautiful properties of numbers and shapes, then we might even begin to see the birth of that "regenerate science" that Lewis prophesied.

The Symbolic Cosmos

The potential reintegration of science with the poetic mode of knowledge is the implicit theme of the next two chapters, where I try to glimpse what was really going on in traditional cosmologies. But we need first to reflect on the nature of symbolism, for without appreciating that we will be unable to find anything worth retrieving in the ancient theories, other than a vague aesthetic appeal.

11. Lewis 1947, 89–90. Cf. Goethe's philosophy of science as described in Bortoft 1996.

12. Taylor 1998, 49.

Poetry and the poetic imagination depend very largely on the interplay of likeness and difference. Simile, metaphor, contrast, analogy, are all used to connect one experience with another. Even the sounds of words are often chosen by the poet to echo the movement or sound of the thing described. In a more subtle sense, images may be chosen to evoke a particular feeling, or even just a quality of attention, as in this famous *haiku* by Basho:

old pond
a frog jumps
the sound of water

This relies on the fact that the reader and the poet have responded in similar ways to such experiences in the past, so that a likeness can be found between the interior worlds of two very different people. The poetic or imaginative appreciation of similarity and correspondence between different things is fundamental to human consciousness, and lies at the root of language itself, as Barfield saw (most of our words are metaphors).

Within this fundamental poetic tradition, specialized studies have evolved. Theology, for example, relies particularly on the method of analogy. Theologians make statements about God, relying on a similarity between Creator and created, despite the overarching difference in the nature of being. In this case the difference is greater than any similarity, but at least something meaningful can be affirmed. We can say God "wishes" or "intends" a particular outcome (such as the salvation of humanity) because the words as applied to human beings *gesture in the direction* of some truth about God, and are endorsed by their occurrence in scripture where God reveals something of himself in terms we can understand

A "symbol" is something that, by virtue of its analogous properties, or some other reason, represents something else. It is not just a "sign," which is made to correspond to something by an arbitrary convention (like a road sign), but has some natural resemblance to what it represents. Traditional cosmologies[13] were ways of reading

13. A "cosmology" in modern science is an account of the universe and its structure. The word may equally be used of ancient and traditional societies, provided we remember that the structure in question was not exclusively a physical one.

the cosmos itself as a fabric woven of natural symbols. The word *symbolon* originally meant something "joined together" and referred to a token, such as a broken ring, which, if matched up with the token's other half, would identify the bearer as a friend. It could therefore mean a code or password used to ensure a message was understood only by those for whom it was intended. It also referred to the articles of faith of a religious community—thus the Nicene Creed is sometimes called "the Symbol of Faith." By extension we can think of a natural symbol such as a tree or a star or a mountain as the visible half of something that also includes a portion not visible to us (such as, in Platonism, the Idea). Thus reading the symbol is a way of passing from the visible to the invisible. Symbols are bridges, making something present to us that would otherwise be absent. In *Sources of the Self* Charles Taylor writes of the Romantic recovery of the importance of symbolism:

> The creative imagination is the power which we have to attribute to ourselves, once we see art as expression and no longer simply as mimesis. Manifesting reality involves the creation of new forms which give articulation to an inchoate vision, not simply the reproduction of forms already there. That is why the Romantic period developed its particular concept of the symbol. The symbol, unlike allegory, provides the form of language in which something, otherwise beyond our reach, can become visible. Where the allegorical term points to a reality which we can also refer to directly, the symbol allows what is expressed in it to enter our world. It is the locus of a manifestation of what otherwise would remain invisible . . . This concept of the symbol is what underlies the ideal of a complete interpenetration of matter and form in the work of art.[14]

Hans Urs von Balthasar has made good use of "symbol" and its equivalents in the development of his theological aesthetics. From Romantics such as Goethe he takes the word *gestalt*, meaning the "figure" that we grasp in knowing a thing—in its highest sense the marriage of the particular and the universal in the eye of the heart.[15]

14. Taylor 1989, 379.

15. Schindler 2004, chap. 3. Schindler explains how *gestalt* is close in meaning to, but not exactly the same as, the Platonic *eidos*, Aristotelian *morphe*, or Scholastic *forma*.

More than the sum of its parts, the figure is the appearing-to-us of an infinite depth that cannot be fully revealed in time. Every symbol is a kind of *gestalt*, in which a universal meaning can be glimpsed. Eventually, every created thing can be seen as a manifestation of its own interior essence, and the world is transformed into a radiant book to be read with eyes sensitive to spiritual light.

To take symbolism seriously is to accept the "analogy of being" between different levels of reality.[16] The context is given in medieval thought by the fundamental analogy between the created order and the uncreated mind of God, but within the created order itself there can be many types of difference, across which analogy links one thing with another. To take the examples mentioned earlier, a tree is a natural symbol of the way the visible (trunk and branches) comes from the invisible (roots and seed), linking higher and lower realities into one living pattern. As such, it can function either as a symbol of the world as a whole (Yggdrasil, in the Norse myths), or of tradition, or of the Church, or of Man. A star by its piercing and remote beauty represents the "light" of higher realities, or the angels, or the thoughts of God, and so on. In each case, these associations are not arbitrary but precise and natural, even to a large extent predictable and consistent from one culture to another (though capable of many applications and variations). The symbol and the archetype to which it refers are not separate things, for the symbol is simply the manifestation of the archetype in a particular milieu or plane of existence. It is "meaning made tangible."[17]

> If . . . the world is the effect of the Divine Word uttered at the beginning of time, then all of nature can be taken as a symbol of a supernatural reality. Everything that exists, in whatever mode, having its principle in the Divine Intellect, translates or represents that principle in its own manner and according to its own order of existence; and thus, from one order to another, all things are linked and correspond with each other so that they join together in a universal and total harmony which is like a reflection of the Divine Unity itself.[18]

16. See, e.g., the discussion of analogy in Cunningham 2002, 181–89.

17. The phrase is from Schindler 2006, 528, an article that eloquently defends Plato from the accusation that he was a dualist who despised the body.

18. Guénon 2001c, 9–10.

This passage is from a modern author, but it accurately captures the traditional view of the world as intrinsically symbolic. I would add only that the harmony of the world reflects the Divine Trinity as well as the Divine Unity, a point I will return to later.

In order to "see" the archetype in the symbol, or "read" it into the symbol, a poetic consciousness is indispensable, which comes more easily to some people than to others. To some it comes not at all, and this is particularly true in the modern world where our education tends to militate against it. But it seems to me not unreasonable to encourage the development of such a consciousness once more, provided we guard against the excesses to which it has always been prone. A superstitious obsession with magical correspondences, or a fascination with the occult, is a corruption of the symbolic imagination. The symbolic sensibility needs to be balanced and integrated with due attention to empirical evidence and logic. But the "prosaic" consciousness is just as subject to corruption in its own way, leading to a brutality and hedonism with which our civilization is only too familiar.

A Key to the Ancient Mysteries

Given what I have said about the meaning of the word "symbol," it is easy to see how any civilization can develop a symbolic language, the elements of which may be partly conventional as well as natural. The art of the Middle Ages was intensely symbolic, and indeed heraldry was one of its branches, where the artist was working within a very diverse but very strict set of conventional significances (each vivid color, each animal, each geometrical form on the knight's coat of arms had a well-understood attribution). But the sculptures and frescoes, mosaics and windows that we find in houses of worship, while freer in some respects than the images of heraldry, are similarly determined by conventional associations, sometimes completely erroneous ones. For instance, the pelican was thought to wash or feed its young with its own blood by piercing its breast, making it an apt symbol for Christ or the Eucharist. But the real-life pelican does no such thing. The lion was thought to sleep with its eyes open, making it a symbol of the eternal vigilance of Christ, and to give birth to pups that lay as if dead until the third day, recalling the resurrection; but again, these ideas were based on travelers' tales rather than careful observation.

In decoding the medieval or ancient symbolic language, one has to bear these conventions in mind. At the same time, one can appreciate that the intention was nevertheless to read nature herself, seeing the mysteries of the faith reflected in the many wonders of the natural world (animals, flowers, minerals, planets), and that these literary embellishments do not invalidate the method or spirit of the symbolic approach. Modern science has discovered many more natural wonders, but we have lost the ability to relate these—however fancifully—to spiritual truth. Books such as Emile Mâle's *The Gothic Image* and Jean Hani's *The Symbolism of the Christian Temple*, Guénon's *Symbols of Sacred Science* and Charbonneau-Lassay's *The Bestiary of Christ* can help us recover this lost language, which is the language of the poetic imagination, condensing multiple meanings into vivid images drawn from nature.

Of all natural symbols, the richest and most eloquent is man himself—the only creature we are told was made "in the image of God" (Gen. 1:27), and who is therefore "the only creature on earth which God willed for itself (*Gaudium et Spes*, 24).[19] In medieval terms, which can be traced back at least to Pythagoras through Philo and others, man is not only an image of God, but an image of the ordered cosmos, a "microcosm" or world in miniature, possessing a balance not only of the four elements and humors, but of spirit and matter. Positioned thus between the material world and the angelic, man (male and female) is a natural mediator and vicegerent of the Creator. Adam's fall displaced him from this position, but in Christ it was restored to him, along with his proper authority over

19. Pope John Paul II offers a profound modern reading of this "language of the body" and specifically the language of gender as expressing our calling to interpersonal communion and self-gift. In this we are marked by the image of God as Trinity. He shows further how theology becomes pedagogy: the gendered body is assigned to man as a task and therefore a spirituality. The development of our biological knowledge at the expense of our consciousness of the body as a "sign of the person, as a manifestation of the spirit," plays into the hands of a dualism that alienates us from our own bodies and reduces them to property (John Paul II 2006, 360–61).

animals and elements—this being displayed miraculously in many of the saints. The animals represent the various human faculties and tendencies, as in a vast external projection, and the True Man is a master over them as he is over himself, being interiorly submitted to God.

Christian symbolic traditions were adapted from those of the ancient world—Mesopotamia, Egypt, Greece—and in many cases these traditions needed little or no change. The real difference lay deeper, in the way symbolism functioned in the new religion. For Christians believed not only that the temporal world was an expression of God's will and wisdom—in something like the way that pagans had believed that it was ruled and shaped by the gods, or that it was a shadow of the world of the Ideas—but that God had entered into that world, using its analogous resemblance to him in order to form it into a vessel for his actual presence.

Jesus Christ was, like Adam, a man who symbolically represented the whole of creation and was an image of God. In fact, since he remained without sin, Jesus was a *perfect* image of God in a way that fallen Adam could not be. However, he was not merely the perfect image of God; he was God. This mysterious entwining of divine and human natures is called the "hypostatic union." It means that grace, and the source of grace, are now within creation as well as outside it, that grace and nature interpenetrate. The whole sacramental system stemmed from this; the symbols incorporated into the sacraments of the Church were not mere reminders of eternal truths, or methods of teaching the uninitiated, but the channels through which grace flowed into the world from Christ.[20] For his divinity connected with all other men and things through his humanity. In that sense the Incarnation set a divine seal upon the poetic structure of the cosmos.

I want now to turn to the symbolic cosmos itself in more detail, bearing in mind that for Christianity it had become the vessel of

20. They were not the only or exclusive ways that grace could reach men, even if many Christians naturally assumed that they were. God could not be bound by his sacraments—hence the possibility that good pagans could be saved, provided they had not knowingly closed their hearts to whatever grace was offered them in their own lives and traditions.

divine presence. We will see that when Western thought lost this sense of the intimate relationship of the natural with the supernatural, it lost even the poetic "pagan" sensitivity to natural symbolism that Christianity had integrated and transformed. Our task today is to recover both.

3

The Lost Wisdom of the World

But thou hast arranged all things by measure and number and weight.

Wisdom of Solomon 11:20

That you, being rooted and grounded in love, may have power to comprehend with all the saints what is the breadth and length and height and depth.

Ephesians 3:17–18

The four disciplines of the *quadrivium*—arithmetic, music, geometry, and astronomy—had one thing in common: they were based in mathematics. Music was the expression of numerical harmonies in time, geometry the exploration of relationships in space, and so on. The assumption of this system of education was that by learning to understand the harmonies of the cosmos, our minds would be raised toward God, in whom we could find the unity from which all these harmonies derive: Dante's "love that moves the sun and the other stars." Thus the *quadrivium* would prepare the ground for the study of the highest contemplative sciences: philosophy and theology.

The idea that the cosmos is built on mathematical harmonies, and that numbers themselves can be a path to God, flowed from Pythagoras and Plato down to the Middle Ages, where it influenced the cathedral builders and later the artists of the Italian Renaissance.[1] It was also one of the essential factors in the birth of science, as we shall see in more detail later, and it continues to influence and intrigue physicists today. Werner Heisenberg writes that "modern physics has definitely decided in favour of Plato. In fact the smallest units of matter are not physical objects in the ordinary sense; they are forms and ideas which can be expressed unambiguously only in mathematical language."[2]

In 1937, another great modern scientist, Paul Dirac, speculated that "the ancient dream of philosophers to connect all Nature with the properties of whole numbers will some day be realized."[3] Heinrich Hertz, the German physicist who demonstrated the existence of electromagnetic radiation in 1888, provides further evidence of the Pythagorean spirit in modern science when he comments: "One cannot escape the feeling that these mathematical formulae have an independent existence and an intelligence of their own, that they are wiser than we are, wiser even than their discoverers, that we get more out of them than we originally put into them."[4]

Michael S. Schneider writes:

> Numbers are a map of the beautiful order of the universe, the plan by which the divine Architect transformed undifferentiated Chaos into orderly Cosmos. Cultures didn't necessarily learn this from each

1. See Joost-Gaugier 2006.

2. Cited in Pickover 2005, 226. According to Paul Friedländer, "Plato's physics of elements being transformed into each other and of regularly divisible atoms was incomprehensible as long as classical physics reigned supreme, i.e., from Newton to the recent past. Now, these chapters of the *Timaeus* have acquired a new meaning, and perhaps Plato may be looked upon as a predecessor of Rutherford and Bohr in the same sense that Demokritos was a predecessor of Galileo and Newton" (257).

3. Cited in Barrow 2003, 102.

4. Cited in Pickover 2005, 229.

> other but only had to *look at numbers and their relationships* to see how they revealed harmonious models which are the same everywhere and at all times.[5]

Yet our present education tends to eliminate the contemplative or qualitative dimension of mathematics altogether, reducing everything to sheer quantity. Mathematics is regarded as a form of logical notation, a mental tool with no relation to truth except the fact that it assists us in manipulating the world. This elimination of the symbolic dimension of mathematics is largely responsible for the divorce of science from religion, and art from science. But rather than continue arguing that case in the abstract, I want to immerse us in an alternative vision of mathematics. Let us learn for ourselves the beauty to be found in this world of patterns and relationships.

Sacred Number

There is something mysterious about numbers. One of the greatest mathematical geniuses of all time, Srinivasa Ramanujan (d. 1920), was able to see the solutions to complex mathematical problems without needing to work them out. He was a devout Hindu and attributed his insights to revelation. He is famous for saying "An equation for me has no meaning, unless it represents a thought of God." Even a materialist must regard numbers as part of "reality," while puzzling over the fact that they are made neither of matter nor energy. He can't observe them through any scientific instrument, yet they somehow underpin everything we see around us and help to define its form.

The Pythagoreans regarded each number as an expression or facet of Unity (the Father of all things) projected through Duality (the Mother) to create multiplicity.[6] The multifaceted nature of number "appears most clearly when one transposes each number into its corresponding geometrical form: three into an equilateral triangle, four into a square, five into a regular pentagon, etc. In each of these

5. Schneider 2006, 81–82.
6. See, e.g., Iamblichus 1988.

figures, innumerable relationships appear, which multifariously throw light on the inner law proper to the figure in question."[7]

The Pythagorean-Platonic tradition at the core of the Liberal Arts developed the following symbolic associations with the natural numbers:[8]

One

The Unity of being, transcending all that exists. It is often represented by a circle, or else by a point. One is the number that when "squared," i.e., multiplied by itself, produces itself. Symbolically, One is not the first in a series of numbers, but the number-beyond-number that includes all others, equivalent in that sense to the modern conception of infinity. There are circular windows in Gothic cathedrals that symbolize this unity, for example at Chartres, Notre Dame, and Rheims.

Two

If one is the source and archetype of Unity, two is the beginning of Diversity. It represents polarity and division, and also feminine receptivity and fruitfulness. In a Christian context it often signifies the separation of matter and spirit. Duality can also symbolize the beginning of the process of creation, which in the book of Genesis is described as taking place through a series of separations or polarizations (heavens and earth, light and dark, etc.). The division of Adam's unity into duality gave us male and female. Geometrically duality appears as a line between two points, or else as the central point and circumference of a circle, joined by a radius.

Three

Unity and Diversity are reconciled in Harmony. The triangle that is the geometrical translation of the fundamental musical chord with its three notes is called a Triad. It presents a graphic image of how the number three returns polarity to unity. The number Three was often regarded as the first real number, after the two principles that were the

7. Burkhardt 1987, 79.
8. Cf. Lundy 2005.

source of number. Plato thought the particles of all natural elements were constructed from triangles (see below). An equilateral triangle is the simplest shape that can be repeated on a two-dimensional plane without leaving any space (just as the tetrahedron can be stacked in three dimensions without leaving space between). As such it is necessarily one of the fundamental building blocks of both art and cosmos. The world and man—macrocosm and microcosm—were both held to be of a threefold nature (matter, soul, spirit). Naturally in the Christian tradition the mark of the Trinity is everywhere. An equilateral triangle inside a circle is sometimes used to suggest the one God in three persons.

Four

Quaternity, expressed as a square, the first "solid" number, represents the earth, or the entire material plane. For the ancients, the world below the stars was composed of four elements: earth, water, air, and fire (perhaps equivalent in modern physics to the four basic states of matter: solid, liquid, gas, and plasma). Earth and fire were opposed to each other (contraction vs. expansion, solidity vs. radiance) while water and air mediated between them. According to Aristotle, there were four types of causation (end, agent, matter, and form). In Christian tradition, there are four rivers of paradise, four senses of scripture,[9] and four evangelists whose foundational writings are spread throughout the four corners of the world.

Five

Five is the marriage of two and three, even and odd, female and male, the mid-point of the Decad, associated with the human body as center of the world. The body has five senses, and five fingers on each hand. Whereas inanimate nature conforms to the order of four- and six-fold symmetry, as in crystal structures, living nature appears to be ordered more often by fives. Five is manifested geometrically as a regular pentagon or a five-pointed star, perhaps more often used in

9. (1) "Literal" or historical-factual, (2) "allegorical" or doctrinal, (3) "tropological" or moral, and (4) "anagogical" or mystical, perhaps corresponding to the four types of causation.

Islamic art than Christian. The pentatonic scale in music is represented by the black keys on a piano. Five has a particularly close relationship to the golden ratio, as we shall see later.

Excursus: The Five Platonic Solids

If you start with a point representing one, extend it into a line representing two, then swing one of the two ends of the line around the other to create a circle representing three, and finally rotate the circle to make a sphere representing four, you have the simplest possible representation of the dimensions of space. It so happens that only five geometrical figures with identical plane faces and equal edges can be made to fit exactly within a sphere. These figures therefore symbolize the complete potentialities of three-dimensional space. They are known as the Platonic Solids, though judging from artifacts in Oxford's Ashmolean museum dating back 4000 years they were discovered long before the Greek philosophers donned their sandals.

Plato hypothesized in the *Timaeus* that the world is made not just of four but of five elements in various combinations. Particles of each element are formed in the shape of one of the five solids—Cube (Earth), Icosahedron (Water), Octahedron (Air), Tetrahedron (Fire), and finally Dodecahedron. The fifth element (to which Aristotle gave the name Aether, though he was uninterested in Plato's geometrical hypothesis) is what God uses to "embroider" the sky with stars.[10] (The Aether was in a sense disproved by the Michelson-

10. For further details see Sutton 2005, and Critchlow 1994. The solids themselves are not the most fundamental elements of nature, according to Plato, since each is composed of equilateral or right-angled triangles. Thus the whole of nature is reduced (or raised) to a triadic principle, through which it is implicitly resolved back into unity.

Morley experiment in 1887, but later tacitly reinstated by Einstein under the new guise of the space-time continuum itself.)

Six

Six is called a "perfect" number because it is the sum as well as the product of its divisors one, two, and three.[11] It is represented geometrically as a regular hexagon, or by the Star of David also known as the Seal of Solomon (two superimposed triangles, one pointing up, the other down). Comprised of six equilateral triangles, the hexagon is the third shape that can be repeated in a plane without leaving any space. If equal sized spheres are allowed to stack along any plane they will form patterns of either six-fold or four-fold symmetry. It is the number of creation (six days), and of the four plane directions plus up and down.

Seven

The days of creation (six days of work and one of rest) are reflected in the seven days of the week. This number appears many times in scripture, being a particular favorite of St. John, for whom it is the number of the Holy Spirit. There are seven sacraments, seven gifts of the Holy Spirit, seven deadly sins, and seven virtues in the tradition of the Catholic Church. Seven represents totality, since it is the sum of four (the number of the material order) and three (the number of the Trinity). Philo calls it the "birthday of the world."[12] It is the largest prime within the Decad—known as the "Virgin" number because it alone does not give rise to any other number between one and ten by multiplication or division. As the combination of a square and a triangle it often appears in the composition of both iconographic and Western naturalistic art. In Jewish tradition it is represented by the seven-branched candlestick

11. As the Greeks also knew, there is only one perfect number between 1 and 10, between 10 and 100, between 100 and 1000, and between 1000 and 10,000 (6, 28, 496, and 8128 respectively). After that the pattern changes, and the next perfect number is in the tens of millions.

12. The writings of the Jewish Platonist Philo of Alexandria (d. AD 50) were preserved by Eusebius and were influential on the church fathers. For his arithmology see Philo 1981, 85.

or *menorah*. According to the book of Tobit (12:15), Raphael is one of the "seven holy angels who present the prayers of the saints and enter into the presence of the glory of the Holy One." An eleventh-century hymn which relates the ratios of the plants to musical tones tells us that "The nucleus (*nodus*) of the universe is the number seven."[13]

Eight

Since the Sabbath or seventh day of creation brought the natural world to completion, that day on which God became man in the womb of Mary to remake the world from the inside is sometimes called the "eighth day." Mary may be identified with the perfection of nature and therefore with the Sabbath, and her son Jesus with the eighth. Similarly the number eight may be identified with the day of Christ's resurrection from the dead, which took place according to the Gospels on the day after the Jewish Sabbath (in this way Sunday, not Saturday, becomes the first day of the Christian week). Eight is represented geometrically as a doubled square, or as a regular octagon. So, for example, the baptistry of the Duomo in Florence is an octagonal building, as are many such buildings throughout Christendom. In a major scale the eighth note, the octave, marks a completion of the scale, a repetition of the keynote, and signals movement to a new level.

Nine

As the product of three multiplied by itself, and at the same time the sum of three threes, nine echoes three (for example, the musical triad), indicating the impress of the Trinity on creation. It features most famously in the nine choirs of angels in the celestial hierarchy of the fifth-century monk who purports to be a convert of St. Paul, Dionysius the Areopagite. There are nine *eleisons* in the traditional Mass. The seven heavens of Babylonian religion, each associated with one of the moving heavenly bodies or "planets" (Sun, Moon, Mercury, Venus, Mars, Jupiter, Saturn), become nine with the addition of the sphere of the fixed stars and, above that, God's eternity.

13. Meyer-Baer 1970, 80, 351.

Ten

There were ten Commandments given to Moses and ten Sephiroth or archetypes from which the world is created, according to Jewish mysticism. The fact that we have ten fingers made it the natural basis for counting systems around the world. The sacred *Tetractys* of the Pythagoreans is the sum of the first four numbers, represented by ten points in an equilateral triangle: one over two over three over four—the "four lettered name" of God equivalent to the Jewish "JHVH." It can be used to construct many different geometrical forms in two or three dimensions, including the five Platonic Solids, and the basic harmonies of music.[14]

Here it is: the ancient "theory of everything," a mathematical representation of God:

•

• •

• • •

• • • •

Twelve

Outside the Decad, twelve is probably the most richly symbolic of numbers. The product of three and four, it is often associated with their sum, seven. There are twelve lunar months in the year, and the heavens have been divided into twelve signs of the zodiac, or major constellations along the path of the sun. The heavenly Jerusalem glimpsed at the very end of the Christian Bible has twelve gates corresponding to the twelve tribes of Israel and the twelve apostles of the Lamb.

The intrinsic relationships of 3, 4, 6, 7, 10, and 12 are all beautifully manifested in one of the simplest geometrical forms, composed of nineteen equally sized circles or circular pebbles. Place one circle

14. "The Tetraktys encapsulates the numbers one, two, three, and four as the fractional lengths of a vibrating string that produces the natural seven-tone musical scale" (Schneider 1994, 335–36). This will make more sense after we look at the nature of harmony in a later chapter.

at the center, and six will fit around it, each touching the others—recalling the six days of creation and one of rest in Genesis. Around that circle of circles, only another circle of twelve circles will fit, the whole six-sided figure containing numerous figures including the Tetraktys itself.

Cardinal Ratzinger explores the biblical account of creation and discovers there the concept of sacred number. For, he says,

> the biblical creation account is marked by numbers that reproduce not the mathematical structure of the universe but the inner design of its fabric, so to say, or rather the idea according to which it was constructed. There the numbers three, four, seven, and ten dominate. The words "God said" appear ten times in the creation account. In this way the creation narrative anticipates the Ten Commandments. This makes us realize that these Ten Commandments are, as it were, an echo of the creation; they are not arbitrary inventions for the purpose of erecting barriers to human freedom but signs pointing to the spirit, the language, and the meaning of creation; they are a translation of the language of the universe, a translation of God's logic, which constructed the universe.[15]

Beyond Pythagoras

Today, mathematicians use different terms to describe various kinds of numbers that the Pythagoreans either did not distinguish, or did not recognize. The *natural numbers* are those they knew. These are derived by counting visible objects: 1, 2, 3, 4 . . . , and the Greeks used

15. Ratzinger 1995a, 26.

letters or pebbles (Latin *calculi*) to represent them. Much later, zero was added as a way of signifying the absence of objects: 0, 1, 2, 3 . . . The invention of zero, like that of the wheel, was one of the turning points in the history of civilization. It radically simplified the process of calculation, since a set of nine symbols could be rearranged to make numbers of any size by attributing a value to their position in the composite (without zero it would not have been possible to distinguish between 45, 405, and 40,050). The number series is extended in either direction from zero to yield the complete set of *integers*, both negative and positive: –3, –2, –1, 0, 1, 2, 3 . . .[16]

Zero, by the way, came from India (where it was placed after 9) and transmitted by the Arabs into medieval Europe (where it was placed before 1).[17] In nature there is no zero.[18] Some writers on number symbolism therefore regard it as an interloper, whose introduction as a placeholder led to the loss of awareness of the symbolic properties of number, and especially of Unity (displacing it from its position at the beginning of the number series), creating a framework for the development of atheism. Robert Lawlor writes, for example:

> The "western" rationalistic mentality negated the ancient and revered spiritual concept of Unity, for with the adoption of zero, Unity loses its first position and becomes merely a quantity among other quantities . . . With zero we have at the beginning of modern mathematics a number concept which is philosophically misleading and one which creates a separation between our system of numerical symbols and the structure

16. Among the integers, the prime numbers are fundamental. These are numbers that are only exactly divisible by themselves and one, and which can therefore be said to compose all other integers by multiplication. They are the building blocks of the world of numbers. The first number, 1, is usually not classed as a prime because multiplying by it does not produce another number. In a sense it is more fundamental than any prime, because it produces and is reflected in every other number.

17. The use of Arabic/Hindu numerals was encouraged by the election of the brilliant mathematician Gerbert as Pope Sylvester II in the year 999, and a century later by the translations of Arabic scientific texts by Adelard of Bath. It was Adelard who brought to Europe the text of Euclid's *Elements of Geometry* in the early twelfth century.

18. Note the concept of "zero point energy" or "vacuum energy" in quantum mechanics (the energy in supposedly "empty" space), which is related to the cosmological constant. The quantum vacuum is not an absolute nothingness.

> of the natural world. On the other hand, with the notion of Unity which governs ancient mathematics, there is no such dichotomy.[19]

Personally, I am not so sure. Zero could also be taken as the ground of being, and a symbol for the return to one. Perhaps the mistake lay not in introducing zero, but failing to read it symbolically.

Integers can be divided as well as multiplied by each other, enabling us to add between each whole integer a series of *fractional* numbers, or ratios: ½, ¼, and so on. These are called "rational" numbers (from the same root as "ratio," referring to the relationship of one number with another). In theory, the quantity of these is indefinite, since we can go on subdividing any one of them as much as we like. Each fraction can also be written in *decimal* notation, where each space from the point represents a leap of magnitude, in this case tenfold. When this is done, every fraction forms a closed or repeating pattern of decimals: 0.25, 6.3333 recurring, and so on. These regular patterns reflect the discrete nature of every rational number. (A similar pattern appears in any rational base: binary, trinary, and so on.)

But this means that, although there is an indefinite number of possible fractions between each integer, they are still discrete. In other words, there are gaps between them, no matter how many smaller fractions we decide to create. For that reason, in between every rational integer and fraction of an integer there is actually room for an indefinite quantity of other numbers, namely all those fractions that do *not* form a closed or repeating pattern. These are called the *irrational numbers.* (Rational and irrational numbers together are called "real numbers.")

If talk of "irrational" numbers sounds abstruse, there are nevertheless many practical implications in everyday life. The solar year, for example, like the lunar month, is not a rational multiple of a day. If it were precisely 365.25 days, as we were told in school, then astronomical events related to the apparent position of the sun would repeat precisely over that period, and the year and the day would be back in step at exactly the same point. "So nothing ever repeats exactly.

19. Lawlor 1982, 19–20.

Calendars therefore have to make compromises, and it is the history of those compromises in different cultures that has led to a plethora of calendar systems."[20]

Irrationals cannot be used to count things, but are encountered in relationships *between* things that can be counted. So if the sides of a cube are one unit long (1:1:1), the diagonal of the cube will be $\sqrt{3}$, and of each square face $\sqrt{2}$. Both are irrational numbers, much used in the construction of Gothic cathedrals. Most famously, the circumference of a circle is irrational compared to its diameter. The name we give to the number of times you can divide the diameter into the circumference is the Greek letter π (*pi*). Like all irrational numbers, when expressed as a decimal, π goes on forever (signified by the three dots at the end): 3.141592 . . .[21] Another famous irrational number is Φ or *phi*, the so-called "golden ratio" that describes a particularly harmonious relationship we will look at more closely in a moment.[22]

It is often claimed that because the Pythagoreans at first believed all numbers to be natural, their discovery of "incommensurables" or irrational numbers was a shock to them, and at first had to be kept secret; in fact, there is a legend that they drowned one of their brotherhood to keep it quiet. For it meant that the world could not be explained entirely on the basis of whole numbers such as those in the sacred Tetraktys. But the "crisis of the irrational"—if there was one (and we have little or no real evidence for this)—was only temporary. Irrationals may not have been expressible as whole numbers or even as fractions, but this was because they were the result of using discontinuous numerals to describe continuous spatial or qualitative relationships. Such indefinable quantities were, however, easy to locate geometrically—that is, in two or three dimensions—and the ancient Greeks did their mathematics pictorially in any case.

20. Stewart 1996.

21. Although this sequence of numbers contains no discernible pattern, it is not random, for if any of its integers were deleted or moved the number would no longer be π.

22. *Transcendental numbers* form a subset of the irrationals, in that they are not even "algebraic": that is, they cannot be expressed by any finite equation using rational numbers (integers) as coefficients. *Pi* and *e* (the exponential constant, the base of natural logarithms) are both transcendental numbers in this sense, whereas $\sqrt{2}$ and Φ are irrational but not transcendental.

A higher-order mathematics (such as the one developed by Eudoxus and rediscovered in the modern period) incorporated them without difficulty.

Irrational Beauty

Let's look more closely at these so-called irrationals, and especially at the famous "golden ratio" or "golden section."

When one thing is compared to another we call the relationship a *ratio* (it is this word from which we derive the word "rationality"). Slightly more sophisticated is a *proportion*, or analogy, which is based on the comparison of one ratio with another (A to B is like C to D), especially when there is a common term linking the two ratios that acts as a mediator between them (A to B is like B to C). The most elegant form of this proportionality is one in which there are just two terms, rather than three: A to B is like B to A + B. This is what is called the "golden" or "divine" ratio, also known as the "extreme and mean ratio," designated Φ or *phi*.

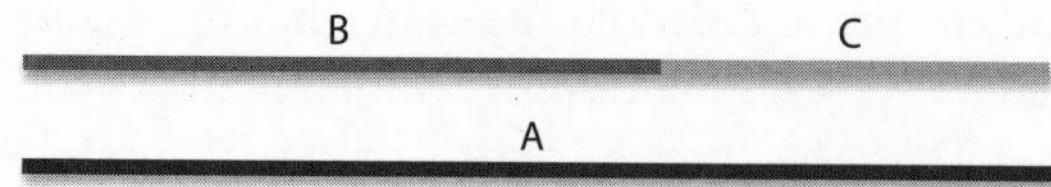

In this diagram, A/B = B/C, and if B is equal to 1, then A = Φ = 1.61804. . . .[23] In other words: if the relation of the larger section to the whole line is proportionally the same as the relation of the small section to the larger, then that relation is Φ. The point dividing the line is called the golden mean.

$$\Phi = \frac{\text{Whole}}{\text{Large part}} = \frac{\text{Large part}}{\text{Small part}}$$

A rectangle is described as *golden* when the ratio between its sides is Φ. If you cut a square out of a golden rectangle, the remaining piece is also a golden rectangle.

23. An endless decimal, because Φ is an irrational number.

Both Leonardo da Vinci and Piet Mondrian used such rectangles frequently in their paintings, and the ratio itself can be found governing the lengths of sections in many Beethoven movements.

Phi is called "Divine" because, like God, it contains within itself both identity and difference. Meditating on Φ and observing it in nature is thought to be a way of raising the human mind toward the divine unity. In his book *Sacred Geometry*, Robert Lawlor relates the golden ratio to both the Trinity and the Logos. *Phi* represents "Three that are Two that are One." He sees this as an exact transcription into mathematics of the words: *In the beginning was the Logos [Word], and the Logos was with God, and the Logos was God* (John 1:1).

> In a sense, the Golden Proportion can be considered as supra-rational or transcendent. It is actually the first issue of Oneness, the only possible creative duality within Unity. It is the most intimate relationship, one might say, that proportional existence—the universe—can have with Unity, the primal or first division of One. For this reason the ancients called it "golden," the perfect division, and the Christians have related this proportional symbol to the Son of God.[24]

Phi "is the perfect division of unity: it is creative, yet the entire proportional universe that results from it relates back to it and is literally contained within it, since no term of the original division steps, as it were, outside of a direct rapport with the initial division of Unity."[25] It is a division that creates difference rather than self-duplication. As a proportion, not strictly a number, *phi* can be taken to represent

24. Lawlor 1982, 46.
25. Ibid., 47. In the paradigm envisaged here, A to B is like B to 1.

the experience of knowledge, or mediation, of analogy—the Logos in all things.

Phi and the Natural Numbers

Phi has a special relationship to the number 5. Not only is it roughly equivalent to 8 divided by 5 (= 1.6), but it is accurately derived from the square root of 5 by adding 1 and dividing by 2. It can also be calculated from the ratio of the lengths between adjacent and alternate tips of a five-pointed star. (Other lines within this figure are divided according the golden ratio: try to work out which ones.)

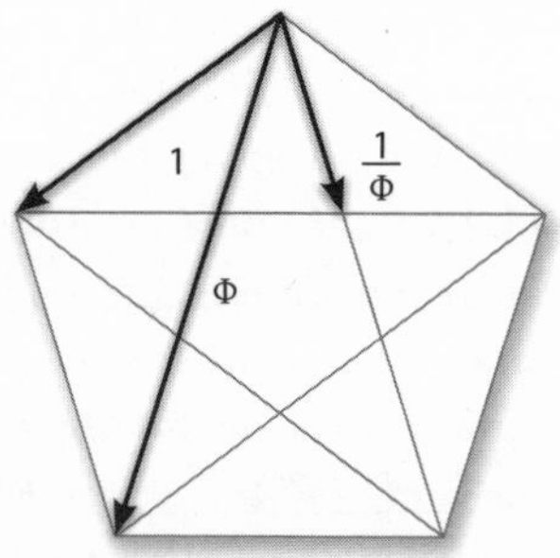

Of course, it is even more closely related to Unity. If you divide Φ into 1, you get a number exactly 1 less than Φ: namely 0.61804 . . . , while if you square it, you get Φ + 1, or 2.61804. . . .

The Fibonacci sequence also approximates to Φ. This sequence, which featured in the best-selling thriller *The Da Vinci Code*, is derived from the work of a mathematician and merchant known as Fibonacci, whose book *Liber Abaci* or "Book of Computation" persuaded Europe to adopt Arabic numerals after AD 1202.[26] The sequence is composed of an open-ended series of numbers starting with zero and one, in which each consecutive set of two numbers added together produce the next: 0, 1, 1, 2, 3, 5, 8, 13, 21, 34, 55, 89, etc. The sequence has many remarkable mathematical properties, apart from the fact that the bigger the number, the closer it approxi-

26. Schneider 1994, 115. Please read the pages that follow in Schneider's book for a full introduction to the golden ratio and its applications.

mates to the golden ratio when divided by the number immediately preceding it. It can also be used geometrically to construct a so-called "golden spiral," in which each turn follows the Fibonacci sequence and *grows from within*—a pattern that seems to recur in galaxies, whirlpools, shells, and plants.

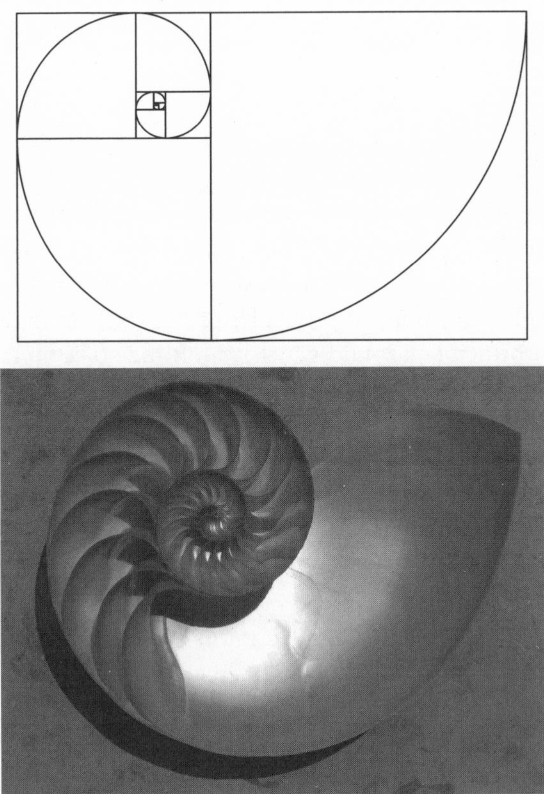

It has often been claimed that this "golden" proportion is one of the defining characteristics of objective beauty, since it is found throughout nature, including the relation of the various parts of the human body (such as the lengths of finger bones or the proportions of the face) to one another. The Greek sculptor Phidias, after whom the ratio is named, is said to have used the proportion in his designs for the Parthenon. The evidence for this is thin, however, and the claim that the ancient architects were familiar with it may have been exaggerated. Quite possibly the presence of the proportion in ancient works such as the Great Pyramid may have been the result of intuition as much as calculation. In the case of the golden ratio, taken up so enthusiastically by artists and architects and even composers after the twelfth century, we may have seen how it is possible not only to reestablish a tradition that the ancients knew well, but to *develop it creatively* in the light of other knowledge.

Symmetry

The same possibility of creative development applies to the tradition I want to mention briefly in the final section of this chapter.

Symmetry, or "patterned self-similarity," has always been treated as one of the fundamental principles of beauty. It is an underlying structural principle, around which a multitude of spontaneous or unpredictable variations can be woven. Such underlying structures are laid bare in mathematics, particularly a branch of mathematics called group theory. Mathematicians tell us that the most basic kind of symmetry is reflectional or bilateral, as seen in the two sides of the human body. A square has four axes of symmetry, because there are four ways to fold it making two equal halves. A circle has infinitely many such axes. Other more complex types of symmetry apply to rotating objects, helices (DNA is a non-repeating helix, thanks to its irrational radians), objects on different scales of magnitude (e.g., fractals), etc.

Transcending the division between rational and irrational, the idea of symmetry can be applied to numbers, shapes, music, words, and ideas. The universe as a whole is highly symmetrical—even more so, it seems, as you wind time backward to the Big Bang. The physical distribution of matter and energy, the laws of conservation of energy and momentum, and even the invariance of physical laws across time and space, are all now seen as manifestations of the same principle, which is why so many popular science books have appeared with titles like *Symmetry and the Beautiful Universe*, *Hidden Unity in Nature's Laws*, and even *Why Beauty Is Truth*.

Once again, we find the ancient intuitions of the Great Tradition borne out in unexpected ways by modern science. The cosmic symmetries exposed by group theory reveal creation as the interplay of the One in the Many. In one of the most helpful of the popular expositions of modern physics, Stephen M. Barr writes,

> Symmetry contributes to the artistic unity of a work, to its balance, proportion, and wholeness. The connection between symmetry and unity is exceedingly important and applies also to symmetry in physics. If one part of a symmetrical pattern or structure is removed, typically its symmetry is spoiled. Cut off one arm of a starfish, and it will no longer have a five-fold but only a two-fold symmetry. Remove one pentagonal facet of a soccer ball, and instead of 120 symmetries only 5 will be left. Symmetry requires all the parts of a pattern to be present, and is therefore a unifying principle.[27]

He goes on to show how the incompleteness of a symmetric pattern often leads to the discovery of a new subatomic particle. In fact all the four basic forces of nature (gravity, electromagnetism, the strong force, and the weak force) are based on and controlled by principles of symmetry, and the "ultimate theory" that is the Holy Grail of physics is currently assumed to lie in the direction of some grand unification of all these four systems of symmetry (as we will see later on).

In a way it could be argued that arithmetic, geometry, astronomy, and music originated in the quest for the ultimate *mandala*: this being the oriental name we give to any symbol of wholeness exhibiting a variety of intensive symmetries, in which each part communicates with and corresponds with every other. A *mandala* is fascinating mainly for its ability to integrate multitudinous variety in a simple pattern. It illustrates one of the most important aspects of beauty: the convergence of extreme unity with extreme complexity. And in such patterns we can see not only the world, but ourselves reflected—or at least ourselves as we aspire to be, images simultaneously of creation and the Creator.

27. Barr 2003, 97–98. Mathematicians now claim to have identified the complete range of possible symmetries right up to a form termed the "Monster," which contains more elements than there are quarks in the sun.

4

The Golden Circle

Mathematics connects directly with theology. If this seems a bizarre notion, it is only because we are so fragmented in our thinking that God and mathematics appear to belong to completely different worlds. If there is to be a revival of the Christian Pythagorean-Socratic tradition along the lines suggested by Pope Benedict, we need to bridge that gap.

In order to make the jump from number to God as understood in the Christian tradition, we have to attune our minds to the idea that God is not just the infinite, or the One, but the infinite *Three*-in-One. One God. Three Persons.[1] What on earth could such a statement mean? Hieromonk Damascene ponders this in his extraordinary work *Christ the Eternal Tao*:

> The Triad contains itself in perfection,
> For it is the first that surpasses the dyad.
> It lies beyond the duality of matter,
> Of subject and object,
> Of self and other.

1. Christian trinitarian doctrine and its history are usefully summarized in O'Collins 1999.

The Triad is beyond the distinction of the one and the many;
Its perfection goes beyond the multiplicity of which duality is
the root.
Two is the number that separates,
Three the number that transcends all separation.
The one and the many find themselves gathered together in
the Three.
For the Triad, being many, is also a Unity:
Not a unity of self-absorption, but of love.

For the Three have one nature, one will, one power, one
operation.
As One, They do not blend or become confused,
But They cleave to each other, having their being in each
other.
This is the perfect love, the original unity, the original
harmony,
the final mystery
To which no human thought has ever succeeded in rising.[2]

A Journey into God

Tradition tells us that the threefoldness of God is not like that of a triangle or a shamrock or any other created thing. It is not the threeness of three objects that can be placed side by side and counted. Threefoldness in this world—in everything we can see—*points toward* divine triunity, but never reaches that far. Yet once we know that God is three Persons, we can see the mark or image or shadow of triunity in things that are made.

We see that mark or echo, for example, in the three dimensions of corporeal space and the three dimensions of time (past, present, and future).[3] Arguably, we see it also in the three notes of the chord, the three grammatical "persons" (I, you, and he), and the three elements

2. Damascene 1999, 63–64.

3. Of course, there are triads and triads. Not all are equally analogous to the Trinity, or analogous in the same respect. For an exploration of symbolic triads across many religious traditions, see Guénon 2001a. For a Christian perspective on this, see Bolton 2005, esp. chap. 3.

of the human being (body, soul, and spirit), corresponding to the three "worlds" (material, psychical, and archetypal). Edith Stein writes:

> The threefold formative power of the soul must be regarded as a tri-unity, and the same is true of the end product of its forming activity: body—soul—spirit. If we attempt to relate this tri-unity to the divine trinity, we shall discover in the soul—the wellspring that draws from its own sources and molds itself in body and spirit—the image of the Father; in the body—the firmly designed and circumscribed expression of the essence or nature—the image of the eternal Word; and in the spiritual life the image of the divine Spirit.[4]

Following Augustine, St. Thomas argues that every creature bears a trace of the Trinity in being created as an individual, having a form, and being related to other things.[5] Even in Islam, a religious tradition that we tend to think of as anti-trinitarian, the greatest Sufi interpreter of the Qur'an, Muhyiddin Ibn Arabi, notes that three aspects of every creature (and especially the Prophet) correspond to a triplicity in the Creator, which he terms Essence, Will, and Word.[6]

We cannot "prove" (let alone understand) the Trinity of God from such evidence, but these phenomena are illuminated for us by the knowledge of faith: that the maker of all is himself triune. Even mathematics is illuminated by it. It is not simply that numbers can be used as symbols. Numbers have meaning—they *are* symbols. The symbolism is not always merely projected onto them by us; much of it is inherent in their nature.

So is there any way to find the "mark of the Trinity" in the domain of numbers itself? You might do it like this. Every natural number

4. Stein 2002, 463.

5. *ST* 1, Q 45, art. 7. Augustine famously finds an analogy to the Trinity in the psychological triad of memory, understanding, and will, to which one might add the corresponding dimensions of culture—*mythos*, *logos*, and *ethos*. For an exposition of the point that Trinity is the most general characteristic of being, see Florensky 1997, esp. 420–24.

6. Al'Arabi 1980, 141, 272. As Toshihiko Izutsu points out, however, for Ibn Arabi the triplicity of the Creator is not a triplicity of the One, which transcends number. The creation is possible because of its *receptive* triplicity that corresponds to an *active* triplicity implicit in the "singleness" (not Unity) of the Absolute (Izutsu 1984, 198–99).

is a multiple of 1. But 1 multiplied or divided by 1 is 1. This makes $1 \times 1 \div 1$ a kind of arithmetical "icon" of the Trinity. It begins with the Father, who generates the Son as his own image without adding anything to the divine nature. The relationship of each to the other is then expressed as a ratio ($1 \div 1$), which symbolizes the Holy Spirit who is the "unity" of Father and Son.[7]

There are more sophisticated mathematical images of the Trinity—one of them is in the golden ratio itself—but this will do for a start. Once you start looking, you can see pointers to the Trinity everywhere—and that is because *Three-in-One* is actually more fundamental to existence even than *One*. For Oneness has no real place for multiplicity, while Trinity does. This doesn't mean that there is multiplicity in the One, but that multiplicity has its root in the One's relationship with itself.

All this may seem a bit abstract, but it is concrete enough to mark important divisions between one religion, one civilization, and another—Christianity and Islam being the most obvious example.[8]

Theology of the Trinity

Moses, when he asked the identity of God, received this reply: "Say this to the people of Israel, 'I AM has sent me to you'" (Exod. 3:14).[9] When theologians talk about the Trinity, what they are trying to de-

7. So "x" symbolizes the generation of the Son, and "÷" the spiration of the Spirit. But this is only a suggestion. Tom McCormick, in private correspondence, has raised the question of what science and mathematics would look like if based upon a trinitarian conception of the number 1, rather than a monolithic unity derived from Greek and Hindu sources.

8. One of the 99 Beautiful Names of God in Islam is *Al-Wadud*, The Loving. Allah loves his creatures, and is loved by them. But there is all the difference in the world between a God who is loving but needs the creation in order to have an object for his love, and a God who *is in himself* love (1 John 4:8). This is not to say that Allah is a different God from the one worshipped by Christians (the word *Allah* is simply the Arabic for "God"), but he is understood differently in the two traditions. Something has been revealed by Christ that is not revealed explicitly in Islam, namely the interior life of God.

9. This is the divine name that is represented in Hebrew tradition by the four letters JHVH.

scribe is a dynamic but trans-temporal Act "I AM" that is the highest essence and source of both Being and Love.

Pope John Paul II expresses the trinitarian mutuality of the eternal Act of love as follows:

> The Father who begets loves the Son who is begotten. The Son loves the Father with a love that is identical with that of the Father. In the unity of the divinity, love is on the one side paternal and on the other, filial. At the same time the Father and the Son are not only united by that mutual love as two Persons infinitely perfect. But their mutual gratification, their reciprocal love, proceeds in them and from them as a person: the Father and the Son "spirate" the Spirit of love consubstantial with them . . . The Spirit is also called Gift.[10]

The French theologian Louis Bouyer tries to define the trinitarian relations in a way that overcomes the longstanding dispute between Catholic and Orthodox traditions concerning the *filioque* clause of the Nicene Creed (that is to say, the question of whether the Holy Spirit proceeds just from the Father, or from the Father *and the Son* as the Latins affirm):[11]

> Everything comes eternally, within God as well as outside him, from the Father alone, the one invisible in himself as St. Irenaeus would say. Everything that can possibly be comes from him in the Son, comes as eternally enfolded within the Son albeit infinitely surpassed by him. But—or because—everything the Father has gives itself, realizes itself by giving itself through the Son so completely . . . everything also returns to him, reascends to him, recapitulates itself in him in the Spirit. The whole divine life is nothing other than Love given eternally, or rather giving itself, but this love lives only in the interchange by which everything flows from the Father through the Son and flows back to him in the Spirit.[12]

10. John Paul II 1985.

11. The Orthodox claim that the insertion of the word *filioque* into official versions of the Creed by the Latin Church was illegitimate—and the more extreme among them even claim that it makes the Catholic notion of God radically different from that of the Orthodox believer.

12. Bouyer 1999, 232.

Michael Aksionov Meerson summarizes the answer of Orthodox theologian Sergei Bulgakov to the *filioque* controversy as follows:

> The Spirit proceeds from the Father neither in general, nor because of some metaphysical necessity, but as the hypostatic movement of love. Thus "the first movement of the Spirit who proceeds from the Father is upon the Son, as the hypostatic love of the Father." But the second movement of the Spirit as the hypostatic love of the Son for the Father is "from the Son to the Father." Thus the eternal "circular movement of the Spirit from the Father by the Son, or in other words, from the Father and the Son," is completed. Since the procession of the Spirit, as with all relations in the Holy Trinity, is timeless, which is to say, without beginning or end, both formulas are justified if taken together.[13]

Finally, Roman Catholic theologian Francois-Xavier Durrwell gives this succinct formulation: "The Tri-unity has two poles, the Father and the Son, and the eternal movement goes from one to the other: the Spirit is this movement which encompasses and unites them."[14]

In Search of the Logos

These attempts by theologians to describe the Christian Trinity almost require us to move from the realm of number to that of shape—from arithmetic to geometry. Number alone is inadequate to define relationship. We have to recall that mathematics begins not just with counting, but also with measuring. To perform an act of measuring one has to do two things. One has to *count*, but one also has to *compare* one thing with another (for example a ruler or measuring tape). These two functions are distinct and fundamental, for counting has reference to pure quantity, whereas measurement is concerned with the realm of extension, determined by form or "quality." Geometry, then, is more than counting. It has to do with a world of more than one dimension, a world that has shape and form.

13. Meerson 1998, 182–83.
14. Durrwell 1990, 44.

In that world, we can try to draw a diagram to capture some aspects of the doctrine of the Trinity. The simplest involves a triangle to show the relationship of the three Persons in God, thus:

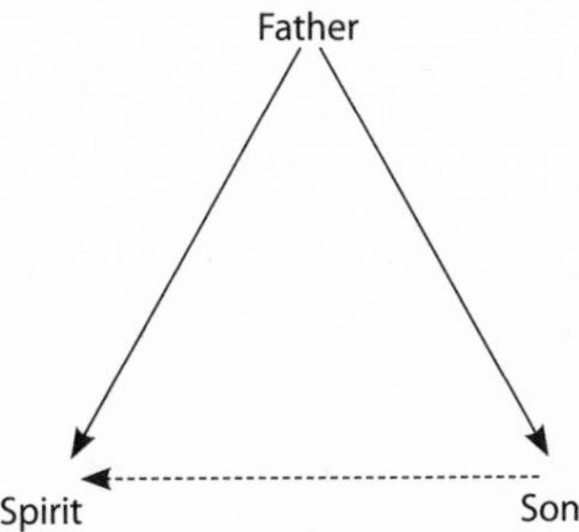

Here we can see the Son and the Holy Spirit coming from the Father. The dotted line represents the Spirit coming also from the Son—this is the *filioque* relationship disputed by the Orthodox. One weakness of the diagram is that there is no indication of any essential difference between the Son and the Spirit. Each is represented by a straight line originating in the Father.

More sophistication can be achieved by combining the straight line with a circle to capture the difference between the Persons: the fact that the Son is "generated" but the Spirit simply "proceeds" or is "spirated" (breathed). Here the Father is represented by a point, the Son by a point extended to form a line, and the Holy Spirit by the circle that joins them together.

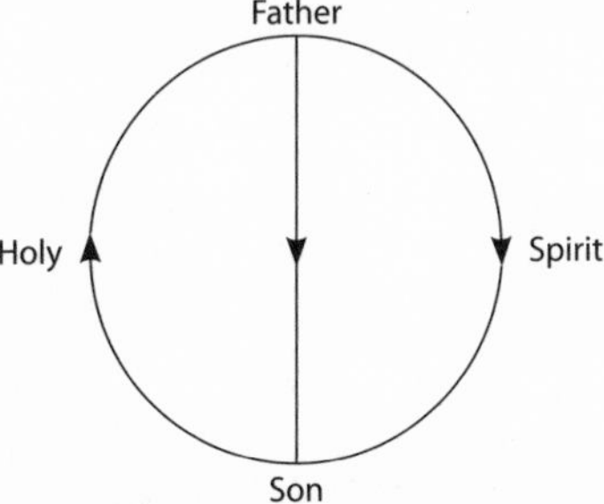

The simple figure of a circle bisected by a straight line is often used to represent the primordial Dyad, the archetypal number Two produced from the One by the act of dividing into two halves. In nature it is seen most clearly in the first division of a fertilized cell.[15] We use it here to represent each divine Person by a different kind of *movement*. The Father is stillness, represented by the point. The Son is linear motion from the Father. The Holy Spirit is circular motion.[16]

So the Father breathes forth the Holy Spirit as a movement that by definition returns to him. The Spirit traverses the same "distance" as the Son (the distance from Self to Other, thus constituting a third, distinct Person), but in a different way, represented by the circle. In a sense it is the Spirit who brings the Son *back* to the Father, in a communion of love that overcomes without destroying the distance of personal distinction. (It might equally be said that the Spirit leads the Son away from the Father before leading him back.) At any rate, the Spirit is one with the Son at his own most extreme departure from the Father, before the curve starts to bend again toward its Origin. The Father, of course, remains "prior" both to Son and to Spirit—not in a temporal sense, but in the sense that the processions are rooted in him alone, as source and fount of the Holy Trinity.

Thus the diagram helps us "encode" the statements that various theologians of both East and West have wanted to make about the Blessed Trinity:

- the Father is the unbegotten Source of Son and Spirit,
- the Spirit originates from the Father as sole principle,

15. A circle bisected by a vertical line is also, coincidentally, the Greek letter *phi* (Φ or φ), which is used in mathematics to describe the first creative division based on Unity (see previous chapter).

16. The direction of the linear motion is irrelevant (it could be up, down, or sideways), so let me put this another way. Imagine a point. The point contains implicitly two forms of motion: the line and the circle. Project each from the point and you arrive at our bisected figure. But there is nothing to prevent the circular motion from extending into every possible dimension. So, with the original point remaining as a fixed anchor, imagine the "disk" formed by the circle swinging around in the same plane to form a larger disk centered on that point. Now imagine this disk swinging around its diameter in the third dimension, to form a sphere. And so on. Whether we represent the Father as the starting point of the smaller circle or as the center of a larger one incorporating it, or even of the sphere that incorporates all possible circles, the fundamental relationships remain the same: the Father as the starting point for both straight and circular motion, representing the Son and the Holy Spirit.

- the Spirit proceeds from the Father,
- the Spirit proceeds from the Father *and* the Son,
- the Spirit proceeds from the Father *through* the Son,
- the Son returns the love of the Father in the Spirit,
- the Son is begotten by the Father in the Spirit.

Geometry as Prophecy

One twentieth-century writer who was adept at translating theology into geometry is Simone Weil, a skilled mathematician (and sister of one of the greatest mathematicians of the twentieth century) as well as a profound religious thinker. Among all those who have studied Pythagorean geometry, she more than any recognized that it is marked deeply by the Trinity, for its central idea is that of mediation (*metaxu*), which she identifies with the Logos (Son). Her approach—introduced, explored, and ably defended by Vance G. Morgan in *Weaving the World: Simone Weil on Science, Mathematics, and Love*—will take us a stage further in the unfolding of symbolic geometry.

For the Pythagoreans, Weil noted, harmony is based on a geometrical mean that establishes the proportion between two different elements. If the two elements are ratios (like musical intervals) that share a common term, they can be fitted together. So, for example, in A/B = B/C, "B" is the mediator or "proportional mean" between the ratios. To use a concrete example, a grandfather is to a father what a father is to his son (where the mediator in this case is the father). Medieval philosophers accounted for all knowledge on the basis of a similar analogy: they said that "knower is to knowing what knowing is to known." A theologian might also say that "God is to Christ what Christ is to man," where the mediator is Christ, who is both divine and human. Weil writes: "'As my Father has sent me, even so I send you, etc.' A single relationship unites the Father to Christ, Christ to his disciples. Christ is the proportional mean between God and the saints."[17]

17. Cited in Ruhr 2006, 46. For more on proportion and harmony, see Critchlow 1994.

Thus to Weil, Greek geometry seemed like "the most dazzling of all the prophecies which foretold the Christ."[18] One recent biographer remarks,

> That most of her contemporary readers will find it difficult to follow her in this, also shows why Weil's reflections on the Pythagoreans are so pertinent to our own times. Apart from telling us something about the genealogy of Christian thought, they invite us to assess the depth of our own conception of the cosmos, show how the loss of a certain perspective may lead to religious belief that is spiritually impoverished, and challenge us to think about ways in which at least a part of that perspective may be regained.[19]

Weil notes that just as mediation from a domain other than number per se, namely geometry, is needed to reconcile incommensurable magnitudes in mathematics, so mediation by a divine Other is needed to reconcile contrary human beings in the world of human relationships: "It is impossible for two human beings to be one while scrupulously respecting the distance that separates them, unless God is present in each of them."[20] For every human being is a self, face to face with others who are also selves. Each of us is the unique center of our own world, an "I." This gulf of absolute otherness can only be overcome with the help of a Third Person, who is the Spirit of love.[21]

> In each of the three relationships indicated by the word friendship, God is always mediator. He is mediator between himself and himself. He is mediator between himself and man. He is mediator between one man and another. God is essentially mediation. God is the unique principle of harmony. That is why song is appropriate for his praise.[22]

The figure of a circular movement bisected by a straight line is probably the most perfect representation we could find of harmony as

18. Weil 1957, 171.
19. Ruhr 2006, 48.
20. Weil 1973, 208.
21. In God, the Father and Son, though one in nature, are also other as Persons. The Holy Spirit eternally overcomes that otherness in a unity that never dissolves the relationship. A married couple become "one flesh" without losing their individual identities, and the presence of the "third" may later reveal itself in a child of the union.
22. Weil 1957, 176.

conceived by the Pythagoreans and raised to its highest power in the Christian Trinity: maximum distance combined with maximum unity between contraries. For Simone Weil, the circle represents God, and the diameter creation, or the "distance" between the divine Persons, within which all things exist: "This universe where we are living, and of which we form a minute particle, is the distance put by the divine Love between God and God. We are a point in this distance. Space, time, and the mechanism that governs matter are the distance."[23]

She then introduces a right-angled triangle into the circle, using the diameter as the hypotenuse (longest side) of the triangle, whose corner lies on the perimeter of the circle. In fact if you project any triangle from the diameter of a circle to its circumference, the largest angle will always be 90 degrees. (Another way of putting this is that a circle is made up of the apexes of an infinite series of right-angled triangles whose hypotenuse is the diameter of the circle.)

Of course, a right-angled triangle has a special significance for the Pythagoreans, as we know from the famous theorem proving that the square on the hypotenuse is equal to the sum of the squares on the other two sides. This implies that the mean of two quantities can always be derived by representing them as the two sides of a right angle. But it is also the case (as Thales showed even before Pythagoras) that the perpendicular line drawn from a right angle touching the circumference back to the hypotenuse will always *equal the mean proportional* between the segments into which it divides the diameter.

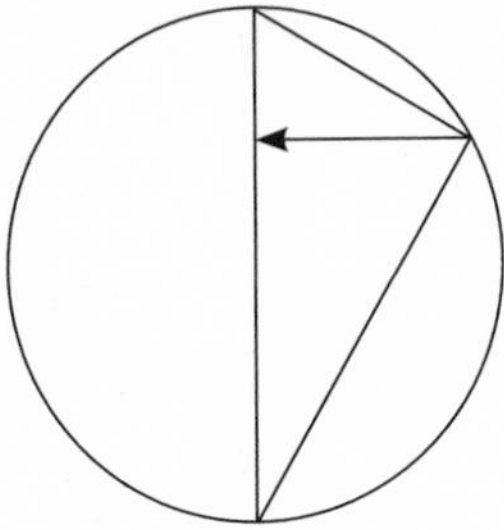

23. From "The Love of God and Affliction," cited in Morgan 2005, 148. Vance Morgan explains that, for Weil, creation's very existence is a suffering and dying motivated by love, and requires an eternal crucifixion of God (147), thus "all geometry proceeds from the Cross."

This fact Weil regarded as perhaps the most beautiful expression of the interplay between circular and linear motion. And into it she reads nothing less than the meaning of the Incarnation, the "God-Man" of Christianity.

> As the circle encloses the moving point upon the diameter, God assigns a term to all the becomings of this world. As the Bible says, He rules the raging of the sea. The segment on the right angle which joins the point of the circle to its projection upon the diameter is, in the figure, an intermediary between the circle and the diameter. At the same time, from the point of view of quantities, it is, like the mean proportional, the mediation between the two parts of the diameter which are on either side of the point. This is the image of the Word.[24]

Here we see the power of the poetic imagination to unite truths that our minds usually keep separate. For Weil, if the circle expresses the infinite motion of God (or the heavens), and the straight line down the middle expresses the world of creation (the earth), then the line linking the circle's perimeter with the diameter at a right angle, the geometric mean, is the world's Mediator, the incarnate Logos.

The Golden Circle

There is more to say about the figure of a circle divided into two halves—into which we have now introduced a right-angled triangle. This next step will require us to draw upon the symbolic properties of the irrational numbers. Let us extend the idea suggested by Simone Weil using Thales's triangle, in which the diameter of the circle projects to the perimeter and a perpendicular is dropped from there back to the diameter, by adding *another* such triangle in the other half of the circle.

These two right-angled triangles, stuck together along any diameter of the circle, make up a rectangle. If we choose the lengths of the sides correctly, we can make it a golden rectangle. That is why I call the figure a "golden circle": it is a circle made golden by the rectangle inscribed within it.

24. Weil 1957, 192. See also Morgan 2005, 113, 144–45.

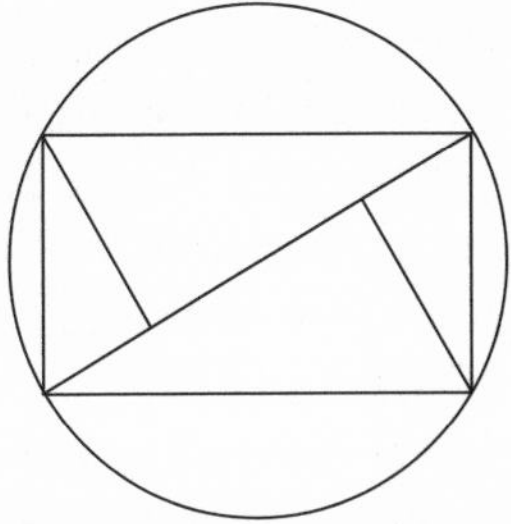

The golden circle is a beautiful synthesis of straight and circular motion, of *phi* and *pi*. The latter, of course, represented by the Greek letter π, is the irrational number (approximately 22/7 or 3.14159) by which the diameter of any circle must be multiplied to find its exact circumference. As the shape of the letter suggests, π is like a "gateway"—in this case between the domain of straight lines and the domain of circularity. We remember that π goes on to infinity when expressed in integers, whether we write it as a fraction or a decimal. In the golden circle, Φ and π are connected together by the fact that the golden rectangle's diagonal forms the diameter of the circle.[25]

If we meditate on this in relation to Simone Weil's circular diagram, in which the diameter represents creation and the circle God, we can see in the infinity of π an expression of the limitlessness of God's act of creation, whenever the divine circular motion gives rise to the straight line of creation.

If we wish, instead of identifying the circle with the divine and the diameter with creation, as Weil does, we could apply the model at a higher level to God as he is in himself—that is, to the Trinity—as we did earlier. In that case the point from which the circle begins or from which it projects is the Father, the line that extends from the point to make the radius or diameter represents the Son, and the circle made by swinging the radius around represents the Holy Spirit. Then π could be read as describing the relationship between the Persons, a relationship that is infinitely fruitful and never ending.

25. By the way, *pi* is related to *phi* by the following formula: $\pi \approx 1.2\,\Phi^2$. The presence of the number 12 divided by 10 is perhaps worthy of note given the ubiquity of 12 as a symbol for the circular cosmos in ancient traditions and 10 as the *Tetraktys*.

Thus the endlessly flowing numbers of π suggest the super-abundance of God's mercy, the infinite quality of his love, and the unlimited space opened up within the Trinity for the act of creation.[26] We see reflected in π the ocean of potentiality, the "waters" over which the Spirit moves at the beginning of Genesis, and into which the Son is projected as a light in the darkness.

But there is another fact about the relationship that is particularly striking. We recall that for Weil the perpendicular is the Logos, linking divinity (the circle) with the created world (the straight line). It turns out by a remarkable coincidence that this "Logos line" is linked to the circle by a number associated above all with the creation of the world by God in the book of Genesis: the number 7. For if we multiply our Logos line by 7 we obtain a close approximation of the circumference of the circle (the exact multiplier is more like 7.025).

Why only an approximation? If it were an exact number that would imply that the "gap" between lines and rectangles on the one hand, and circles on the other, could be bridged without going through the transcendental π. In that case the problem of "squaring the circle" (see next chapter) could easily be solved. But the reason it *cannot* ever be solved in that way is that, as Michael S. Schneider writes,

> true pi reaches for the infinite and never fully engages with things mundane and rational. The transcendental and rational, Heaven and Earth, can approach each other but cannot, by definition, fully meet, as they shouldn't. No ruler and compass construction can truly square a circle. When the divine Architect separated Heaven and Earth it was permanent.[27]

But it seems to me there is another reason why this number is only approximate, and this reason touches on the deepest mystery revealed by Christianity. Mediation between heaven and earth is accomplished by the seven sacraments issuing from the actions of the Logos during

26. The mathematician Clifford A. Pickover argues somewhat fancifully that "somewhere inside the endless digits of π is a very close representation for all of us—the atomic coordinates of all our atoms, our genetic code, all our thoughts, all our memories" (2005, 300).

27. Schneider 2006, 40; cf. Lawlor 1982, 74–79.

his life on earth, echoing the seven mystical days of creation.[28] But we have just found that the "Logos line" needs to be multiplied by a number *very slightly more* than seven to arrive at the Divine Circle. Reading this fact theologically, it seems justifiable to speculate that it is because the mediation of the God-Man will always leave room for the vital but infinitesimal human contribution, our free cooperation with grace.

As St. Paul says: "Now I rejoice in my sufferings for your sake, and in my flesh *I complete what is lacking* in Christ's afflictions for the sake of his body, that is, the Church" (Col. 1:24, my emphasis). This sentence has often been taken by theologians to refer to our cooperation with God in our own salvation and deification (although admittedly I have never before seen a mathematical representation of it). As the Catholic *Catechism* puts it: "God grants his creatures not only their existence, but also the dignity of acting on their own, of being causes and principles for each other, and thus of cooperating in the accomplishment of his plan."[29] It is represented in the Catholic Mass by the drop of water with which the priest slightly dilutes the cup of wine that is about to become the blood of Christ. This is the tiny and indispensable human contribution needed if heaven is truly to descend to earth, and earth finally to be integrated with the everlasting Trinity.

Speculations like those I have mentioned in this chapter will appear forced to many. Yet we must return to the central idea that God's archetypal forms or Ideas are inevitably found within nature at every level, reflected with greater or lesser degrees of accuracy. That is not pantheism but Christian Platonism, perfectly compatible with the insights of theology and the revelations of scripture.

28. See Caldecott 2006, chap. 6.

29. *Catechism of the Catholic Church*, par. 306. It is hard to resist mentioning other examples of a slight difference from 7 that become significant if we read them with an eye to this theological mystery of the incommensurability of heaven and earth. Michael Schneider has pointed out in private correspondence that if you add $\sqrt{2} + \sqrt{3} + \sqrt{5} + \Phi$, the total also comes close to 7—in fact to something like 7.0003. The first three of these irrational numbers, which are also the first three primes, symbolically represent (respectively) Generation, Formation, and Regeneration (see Lawlor 1982, 31), while Φ represents growth, as in the Fibonacci sequence. Together they give a very good description of what the sacraments are supposed to be and accomplish supernaturally in man. It seems fitting then (at least to someone who believes there are necessarily seven sacraments!) for their total to approximate 7. Another example occurs in music, and is known as the "Pythagorean comma" (see next chapter).

5

"Quiring to the Young-Eyed Cherubims"

> For man is in receipt of a singular prerogative beyond all other animals, to worship the Existent, but heaven is ever making music, producing in accordance with its celestial motions the perfect harmony.
>
> Philo of Alexandria[1]

If mathematics is inherently theological, it is also mystical. Writing of the contemplative function of symbolic mathematics, Simone Weil says in her *Notebooks*: "Only such a mystical conception of mathematics as this was able to supply the degree of attention necessary in the early stages of geometry."[2]

As we have seen, the "Liberal" Arts are precisely *not* "Servile" Arts that can be justified in terms of their immediate practical purpose. "The

1. Philo 1981, 115.

2. Weil 1956, 2:512. For Weil prayer consists of attention to God and the concentration required to solve (or even attempt) mathematical puzzles is never wasted, since it develops the soul's capacity for the higher attentiveness—not to mention (in the case of those of us who find mathematics difficult) humility!

'liberality' or 'freedom' of the Liberal Arts consists in their not being disposable for purposes, that they do not need to be legitimated by a social function, by being 'work.'"[3] As Josef Pieper argues, the reduction of the liberal to the servile arts would mean the proletarianization of the world. At the heart of any culture worthy of the name is not work but leisure, *schole* in Greek, a word that lies at the root of the English word "school." At its highest, leisure is contemplation. It is an activity that is its own justification, the pure expression of what it is to be human. It is what we do. The "purpose" of the *quadrivium* was to prepare us to contemplate God in an ordered fashion, to take delight in the source of all truth, beauty, and goodness, while the purpose of the *trivium* was to prepare us for the *quadrivium*. The "purpose" of the Liberal Arts is therefore to purify the soul, to discipline the attention so that it becomes capable of devotion to God; that is, prayer.

Having said all of that, we have also seen that there are indeed a myriad practical applications and implications of symbolic mathematics. I suggested in the second chapter that to appreciate the aesthetic and symbolic dimension of numbers and shapes would be the first step in transforming science itself, that most practical of human pursuits. The recovery of a contemplative appreciation of numbers and shapes would also herald a renewal of the arts (painting, sculpture, music, architecture, even film). For it is the contemplative dimension that connects us with the source of inspiration and beauty in the cosmos and our own souls.

Let us now look more closely at the concept of *harmony* that is central in the Pythagorean tradition—illustrating this in terms of music, architecture, ecology, and astronomy.

Good Vibrations

Every material object is capable of vibrating, and furthermore has a "natural frequency" at which it does so, determined by its physical constitution—in fact most have several such frequencies, called "natural harmonics." Thanks to the phenomenon of resonance, whereby the vibration of one thing sets going a vibration in another, the vibration of (say) a guitar string communicates itself to the air and creates a

3. Pieper 1998, 22.

sound wave that we can hear, because the eardrum starts to resonate in sympathy with it.

Harmony—the perceived agreement or "concord" between different frequencies—was first analyzed mathematically by Pythagoras. He noticed that the sounds made by different hammers hitting an anvil depended on the relative weight of the hammer, and that the sounds seemed to fit together in a pleasing way when the respective weights were in certain ratios to each other (so, for example, when one hammer was exactly twice as heavy as another). The lowest note (or pitch) produced by an instrument such as a string or hammer, or a column of air in the case of a wind instrument, is called its fundamental frequency or "first harmonic." The wavelength of this note will be exactly twice the length of the string. By shortening the string, or holding it partway along its length, another harmonic is produced. In fact any string will naturally vibrate first as a unit, and then in halves, thirds, quarters, and fifths—producing a series of "overtones."

The difference in frequency between one pitch and another is called an "interval," the "octave" being the name given to the interval separating the first and second harmonics (2:1).[4] Within the octave the Western classical tradition recognizes seven intervals in a major scale: "unison," "second," "third," "fourth," etc. up to "seventh," each slightly bigger than the one before:

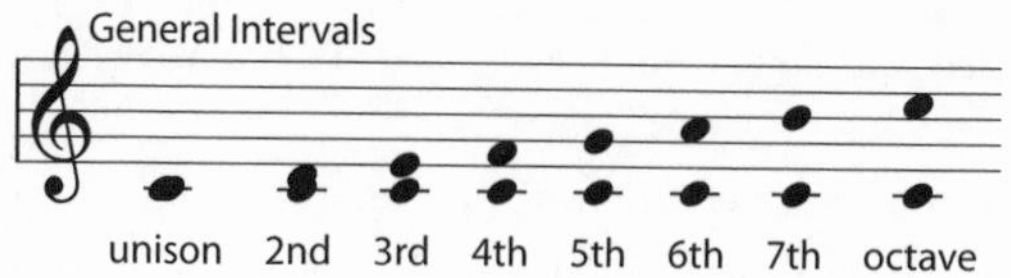

Notes that are in whole-number ratios to each other sound good together. These ratios can be displayed visually by an instrument called a harmonograph, in which each vibration is conveyed by pendulum to a pen and paper. Harmonic or resonant patterns can also be displayed

4. It is called "octave" because the classical scale was divided into seven notes. By raising the pitch from one note to another you could progress through the scale contained between the first and second harmonics. The eighth step up would commence another octave, just as the eighth day of one week is the first of the next. (Similar principles seem to apply to color, for just as our ear naturally distinguishes seven notes in a scale, our eye tends to distinguish seven colors in a rainbow.)

on a plate covered in sand that is made to vibrate at certain frequencies by being connected to a sound system. Either way, sounds made by notes that harmonize together turn out to be visually, as well as audibly, beautiful:

Chladni patterns produced by sand on a vibrating metal plate.

For the Pythagoreans the whole universe was composed of a single "octave," the interval between 1 and 2, Unity and Diversity, Monad and Dyad. The musical scale was thus nothing less than a model of the cosmos, and could be analyzed mathematically in a way that confirmed our intuitive response to beauty.[5]

5. Platonists following the *Timaeus* expressed this model in the form of the Greek letter *lambda* (Λ). At the top they placed unity, source of all other numbers, with immediately below that the first even and first odd, followed by squares and cubes corresponding to the first, second, and third dimension of space: line, plane, and solid.

1
2 3
4 9
8 27

From the ratios between these seven fundamental integers they could deduce (by taking the arithmetic and harmonic means of the numbers) musical consonances, the music of the heavens, and the harmonies of the soul.

In the twelfth century, at the cathedral of Notre Dame in Paris, a musical revolution took place expressing the genius of the new Gothic architecture in the world of sound: the monastic plainchant, with its single line of text, became polyphonic. Now two or even four different voice parts could overlap and interweave, making harmony together. This added whole new dimensions to the sound, and made possible an explosion of creativity in music that has still not exhausted itself. Written notation was developed to enable the singers to record and transmit their new harmonies more easily, and thus the revolution quickly spread throughout Christendom. As part-music reached a new level of complexity, the question of timing became increasingly important, leading to measured rhythm and new conceptions of musical form.

As plainchant and drone gave way to polyphony and chords, Pythagorean music theory evolved too. The sixteenth century divided the octave into twelve exactly equal parts (called the chromatic scale) to make it easier to tune an instrument. It eliminated the so-called "Pythagorean comma," a discrepancy—like those mentioned at the end of the last chapter—that occurs when tuning in perfect fifths (3:2 intervals). Twelve perfect fifths are almost but not exactly equal to seven perfect octaves, and the Pythagorean comma is the amount of the discrepancy. They can therefore be treated as the same interval by flattening (tempering) each fifth by a twelfth of a comma.[6]

Mathematically the octave, the fifth (five notes up from the note of the whole string), and the fourth (four notes up) are said to be the purest intervals, while the most consonant or harmonious are unison, of course (because it has a frequency ratio of 1:1), the octave (2:1), the major third (5:4), and the major sixth (8:5). Some say that the most beautiful interval is the major sixth, which, it will come as no surprise, happens to be a close aural approximation to the golden ratio (8/5 = 1.6).

The word "music" has acquired a rather more restricted meaning than it once had. Today we think of a musical piece as a piece of writing, whose author is known and which is generally performed for

6. The "comma" seems to correspond to the discrepancy between the months of the solar and lunar calendars, and so may have been taken to represent a distinction between heavenly and earthly harmony. See Barker 2003, 275–76.

aesthetic pleasure in a concert-hall setting. Music has been mechanized and packaged in ways typical of our society. As we saw earlier, among the Greeks the "art of the muses" enfolded the whole of intellectual and literary culture (as opposed to the physical culture of gymnastics), while even in its narrower meaning it included dance and poetry as well as singing and the playing of instruments. As such it was not a specialized study but a vital part of all humane learning, as well as being closely related to its companions in the *quadrivium*, arithmetic, geometry, and astronomy.

Polyphony did nothing to undermine that broader and deeper understanding of music that we see, long before the golden age of Western classical music, in Hugh of St. Victor's *Didascalicon* (c. 1130), where his chapter on the subject begins: "The varieties of music are three: that belonging to the universe, that belonging to man, and that which is instrumental." And he elaborates:

> Of the music of the universe, some is characteristic of the elements, some of the planets, some of the season: of the elements in their mass, number, and volume; of the planets in their situation, motion, and nature; of the seasons in days (in the alternation of day and night), in months (in the waxing and waning of the moons), and in years (in the succession of spring, summer, autumn, and winter).[7]

It is assumed here that to understand the universe is to appreciate its music, the harmonies between its parts, the rhythm of its movement, and the proportion of its elements. (The teaching goes back to Ptolemy's *Harmonics* in the second century, and of course to Pythagoras before him.) So too for what today we would call psychology and medicine: "Of the music of man," he says in the same place, "some is characteristic of the body, some of the soul, and some of the bond between the two." Music is characteristic of the body in its "vegetative" power (the power of growth), as well as through its composition and activity. It is "characteristic of the soul partly in its virtues, like justice, piety, and temperance; and partly in its powers, like reason, wrath, and concupiscence." Finally,

7. Hugh of St. Victor 1991, 69.

> The music between the body and the soul is that natural friendship by which the soul is leagued to the body, not in physical bonds, but in certain sympathetic relationships for the purpose of imparting motion and sensation to the body. Because of this friendship, it is written, "No man hates his own flesh." This music consists in loving one's flesh, but one's spirit more; in cherishing one's body, but not in destroying one's virtue.[8]

Since the twelfth century Western tonal music has evolved in so many directions that today it can be said there are as many kinds of music as there are moods and aspirations of the human heart. But perhaps it is still possible to find some underlying principles in the nature of man, as Hugh suggests with his attempt to relate different types of music to the different levels of the human organism. In the final chapter I will come back to the question of anthropology and the three fundamental levels we need to consider in this connection: body, soul, and spirit. Different sounds resonate in different parts of the body, so the natural symbolism of musical sound is related to the symbolism of the body itself, with the higher and purer notes often representing spiritual aspiration (even when played on the electric guitar), the lower bass notes connecting us more with the earth. There are styles of music that appeal to each of the three levels, and within each style or genre there may be an upward or a downward tendency. Rhythm connects us with the cycles of time and of biological life, while melody and lyrics, dynamics and texture evoke other ideas and associations across the whole range of human experience.[9]

There is also a close parallel between sound and light. In Sanskrit the roots of the words for "shine" and "sound" are the same, and in modern physics both are forms of vibration. Haydn linked each instru-

8. Ibid.

9. Recent research suggests human beings may be unique among animals in having a sense of rhythm, learning to synchronize their movements with an auditory beat. Neurologically this might be explained by a connection between the part of the brain concerned with movement and that concerned with hearing. No doubt an evolutionary reason can be invented to account for this. But the same facts can be "read" from the other side as expressing a metaphysical truth about man, whose attunement to the cosmos is part of his nature and necessary to his purpose.

ment in the orchestra to a distinct color (the trumpet scarlet, the flute sky blue, and so on), and Messiaen attempted musically—some would say unsuccessfully—to evoke the "perpetual dazzlement" of heaven and the New Jerusalem (Rev. 21:2, 10–27) that he glimpsed through the stained glass of St. Chapelle, describing his sonic language as intended to evoke a "theological rainbow."[10] It is for this reason too that J. R. R. Tolkien represented the creation of light in his mythological story "Ainulindalë" as a making-visible of angelic music. There are mysteries here that we need to explore further.

According to the English composer John Tavener (b. 1944),

> all music already exists. When God created the world he created everything. It's up to us as artists to find that music. Of course that's an exhausting experience, but you have to rid yourself of any preconceived idea about what music is; rid yourself of the idea that you *have* to struggle over note rows, or with sonata form, or the humanist bugbear, development. Music just is. It exists. If you have ears to hear, you'll hear it! . . . I believe we are incarnated in the image of God in this world in order for us to re-find that heavenly celestial music from which we have been separated. Our whole life is a continuing return to the "source." The fact that modernism can envisage no source is a very grave and catastrophic state of affairs.[11]

Tavener, of course, is a purist, and is, besides, talking mainly of sacred music. He believes that chant "is the nearest we can get to the music that was breathed into man when God created the world."[12] It must be sung, because "music is the extension of the Word, not a frilly decoration of the Word," and ideally (according to the Greek Orthodox Church which influenced him at this time) "there must be no harmony, no counterpoint, just a single melodic line with an *ison*, or the tonic note of the melody, representing eternity."[13] In fact he is not necessarily advocating a "return to chant," but stressing our need

10. Cited in Begbie 2008, 169. Jeremy Begbie's book is recommended for the reader who wants to investigate the religious dimensions of music.

11. Tavener 1999, 73–74, 98.

12. Ibid., 135–36.

13. Ibid., 48.

to learn from chant, and to aspire to produce again a kind of music that is transparent and timeless in that way.

Humane Architecture

For Hugh and the medievals, the ultimate concern of music, as of all the arts, "is with the changeless archetypal patterns in the divine Wisdom, to whose likeness the arts restore man."[14] Similar principles apply in the field of architecture. The conditions that make modernist architecture mechanistic and inhuman—in a word, ugly—are rooted in a philosophy of life that architects, by and large, have absorbed, accepted, and perpetuated along with everyone else.

You can see the problem while walking around any ancient city like Oxford, with its buildings of many periods and styles. What I will call "modernist" buildings (because they make a virtue of being modern, and therefore deliberately break with traditional principles of design) tend to be those which resemble concrete boxes, blockhouses and bunkers, or are composed of rectangular plate glass over metal and concrete frames. Children, with their fresher eyes, can recognize the ugliness of this kind of building when we adults sometimes cannot. But even when the buildings are made of brick or stone, the mean or gaping windows and the flat roofs of the modernist building give the game away.

One way of describing what happened to architecture is that the vertical dimension was devalued, or else that the link between the vertical and the horizontal had disintegrated. For there is a natural cosmic symbolism associating the vertical with the spirit, the horizontal with matter. The sky transcends us, the light from heaven illuminates us, the breezes from the sky refresh us, and the gales threaten our destruction. On the other hand, the horizontal is the dimension in which we walk, in which we reach out and touch the world around us, in which we exert our own dominion. These two dimensions are integrated in the human body, which as the medievals rightly perceived forms a "microcosm," a compact representation and sampler of the cosmos as a whole. We stand upright, and this very posture hints

14. Jerome Taylor, in a note to Hugh of St. Victor 1991, 196.

at our potential role as mediator or high priest of creation. We are divided symmetrically between left and right, because the horizontal is the world of division. Within the body, it is the face (and especially the eyes) that represents the soul.

In the first century BC, many of the classical traditions based on the symmetry and proportions of the human body were codified by Vitruvius. (His book was rediscovered in 1414 and had an enormous influence on the Renaissance.) In modern times, with the rise of rationalism and materialism, the transcendent or vertical dimension was neglected as we concentrated on mastering the world around us. At the same time, the significance of the human image was forgotten and man was regarded increasingly as no more than an animal, to be studied by the methods of science. Once these attitudes and assumptions had sufficiently penetrated the popular mentality, architects (along with other kinds of artists and designers) began to create buildings that reflected the modern understanding of man and the world; that is, machines for living in, spaces designed to facilitate efficient motion in a horizontal plane.

Though buildings now reached higher than ever before, skyscrapers were simply horizontal spaces piled one on top of another, with none of the mechanically replicated floors bearing much of an intrinsic relationship to the elevation in which they dwelt. The rectangular designs of the World Trade Centre and the UN building in New York were based on the mechanical repetition of one floor on top of another.[15]

In general, buildings that are flat tend to strike us as drab and ugly, while buildings with peaked roofs, with triangles and curves that connect the horizontal with the vertical, are felt to be more beautiful.[16] Decoration magnifies the effect. Proportions in windows and doors

15. Things are, of course, more complicated than this, and Manhattan's Chrysler and Empire State owe their iconic status partly to the fact that they do possess a form and decorative features that speak of integration and thus of beauty. Le Corbusier's design for the United Nations building, like much of his work, was based on the golden rectangle. Even the Trade Center did not lack a certain beauty (the beauty of a machine or a crystal), though less related by its proportions to the human body than the large buildings of earlier civilizations.

16. Again, a qualification is necessary. In many parts of the world, especially in hot climates, we see that flat roofs can be beautiful too, but there I would claim the

and their settings that echo the shape of the human form, and windows set into recesses or covered with arches that faintly echo the pattern of the eyes within the face, seem "right" to us because they speak at a deep level of the connection between the human person and the world as a whole. The materials of which we make our buildings are just as eloquent. Traditional materials such as wood, stone, or clay speak an immediate connection with the earth. On the other hand, concrete and cement by their very nature represent the brutality of modernism—the reduction of the world to particles in order to force it into shapes of our own devising. The shaping of concrete is done from the outside, by the imposition of mechanical force, rather than from inside by growth or natural accretion.

If we look at a modern city in this way, its underlying philosophy becomes more evident. It is a place where too many obvious features express the desire to control and manipulate, to herd and standardize. The human eye is held on the horizontal plane mainly in order to expose it to advertisements for things we might buy, and it is raised above that plane only to remind us that we are dwarfs in the face of technological power.

One of the aims of the European Enlightenment was "*mathesis*," or the spatializing of all knowledge, mapping the world onto a notional "grid" so that it could more easily be measured and controlled—effectively reducing the world to pure quantity.[17] With this went the attempted substitution of a concept of space for the concept of eternity, and with the attempt to achieve through frenetic activity or movement in space what can only really be attained through contemplation. Aspirations of this sort tend to be implicit in most drives toward greater efficiency, and lie at the root of the sense of ever-increasing stress and shortness of time with which modern man is afflicted.

Our contemporary cityscapes can be traced to a profound philosophical shift in Europe after the fourteenth century. Known as the *via moderna* (probably the first use of the term "modern"), the new-style nominalist philosophy associated particularly with Oxford's Duns

---

instinctive or traditional design of these buildings tends to make use of the vertical dimension in other ways, rather than simply ignore or suppress it.

17. Pickstock 1998, chap. 2. Cf. Guénon 2001b and Guardini 1998.

Scotus and William of Ockham located meaning and order not in the objective but in the subjective realm. Without the mediation of a world-order rooted in divine wisdom, the order of intelligibility had to be imposed on nature by the human mind. From being primarily receptive to reality, we gradually came to see our intelligence as constructive, as though the structure of the world depended on the way we saw and named it.[18]

Though I have referred to religious concepts, I have not yet been talking of sacred or church architecture, but only of the secular architecture that one might find on any street corner. The practical implications were summarized in 1989 by HRH Prince Charles in a book called *A Vision of Britain*.[19] His ten perennial principles for good architecture and town planning based on the concept of service and a sensitivity to the human meaning of buildings were as follows:

1. *Place*. By this he meant be sensitive to location and setting. One place is not the same as another. "Don't rape the landscape."
2. *Hierarchy*. The composition of a building should lead the eye to its most important elements. "If a building can't express itself, how can we understand it?"
3. *Scale*. "Buildings must relate first of all to human proportions and then respect the scale of the buildings around them."
4. *Harmony*. "Sing with the choir and not against it."
5. *Enclosure*. "A community spirit is born far more easily in a well-formed square or courtyard than in a random sampling of developers' plots."
6. *Materials*. "Let where it is be what it's made of."
7. *Decoration*. "We need to reinstate architecture as the mistress of the arts and crafts."
8. *Art*. "Sculpture and painting play an essential role in conferring on public buildings their unique social and symbolic identity, which architecture alone cannot."

18. Louis Dupré's *Passage to Modernity* gives a brilliant analysis of all these developments.

19. Charles 1989, 76–97.

9. *Signs and Lights.* "We should bury as many wires as possible and remember that when it comes to lighting and signs the standard solution is never enough."
10. *Community.* "Let the people who will have to live with what you build help guide your hand."

If we now focus more specifically on sacred buildings, we find that Michael S. Rose has attempted a summary of the principles of church architecture, reducing them to three in particular, which he calls *Verticality*, *Permanence*, and *Iconography*.[20]

In the case of Verticality Rose believes that "the massing of volumes upward . . . most readily creates an atmosphere of transcendence and, in turn, enables man to create a building that expresses a sense of the spiritual and the heavenly." I would add that monumental scale is not an essential element in this "massing." What is essential is that the natural symbolism of the vertical be taken into account, and that the vertical is used to add something qualitative, not merely quantitative, to the form of the church. Gothic architecture achieved its effects by a combination of height and light, evoking by its pointed and interlacing arches and columns the atmosphere that one might find beneath an ancient forest canopy, or within vast caverns under the earth. Byzantine architecture has a different feel entirely, even when the spaces within the building are huge. Here the heavens are closer, indeed seem almost wrapped around the worshipper. Either heaven has been brought to earth, or we have been raised to heaven. But both styles use space to express a theology.

The second of Rose's principles, Permanence, involves a similar use of the "fourth dimension," time. The transcendence of time by eternity, and by Christ as the incarnation of eternity in time, is suggested by the stability and durability of the church. An effective church building is a manifestation of tradition, and tradition is more than just the dead accumulation of custom; it is a living organism that overcomes time and death by a process of continual regeneration and gradual creative development. The church building, if it achieves permanence

20. Rose 2001, 15–29. He compares these to the traditional principles of Utility, Strength, and Beauty.

simply by resisting change and being preserved over centuries, might be no more than a museum or monument. But if it is built to last and is *sustained from within by a community of worshippers* then its permanence becomes a true reflection of eternity.

The third law of church architecture is Iconography, by which Rose means the capacity of the building to convey meaning not only by its overall form, but by the details of its composition and adornment. From the range of Christian iconography one should not exclude the whitewashed elegance of some Protestant and Nonconformist chapels, but what Rose has in mind primarily is the rich heritage of mosaics, frescos, stained glass, panels, and statues that are to be found in Catholic and Orthodox churches. Here again style, which is the organic expression of a living tradition, manifests theology.

Some years before his election as Pope in 2005, Benedict XVI wrote of the development of Christian iconography as follows:

> But now the idea awakens in Christianity that precisely God's incarnation was his entry into matter, the beginning of a momentous movement in which all matter is to become a vessel for the Word, but also in which the Word consistently has to make a statement about itself in matter, has to surrender itself to matter in order to be in a position to transform it. As a consequence, Christians are now deriving pleasure from making faith visible, from constructing its symbol in the world of matter. The other basic idea is connected to this: the idea of glorification, the attempt to turn the earth into praise, right down to the stones themselves, and thus to anticipate the world to come. The buildings in which faith is expressed are, as it were, a visualized hope and a confident statement of what can come to be, projected into the present.[21]

Church architect Steven J. Schloeder has discussed the "Church as Icon" in his book, *Architecture in Communion*. A church by its very nature is a symbolic structure, and that symbolism potentially includes its cosmic situation, its orientation in relation to the sun and stars,[22] as much as the details of its workmanship and decoration both inside and out. A church is intended to be read like a book—to evoke and provoke contemplation, which is the inward journey. Unfortunately,

21. Ratzinger 1996, 88.
22. See Ratzinger 2000, 62–84; Lang 2004.

modern man has largely lost the ability to turn the pages, let alone read the language of symbolism.

In the case of the Gothic, a deliberate attempt was made by its twelfth-century inventor, Abbot Suger, to incarnate the vision of the New Jerusalem from the twenty-first chapter of the book of Revelation.[23] Precious stones were placed in the walls, and the overall impression of light flowing through the huge windows was designed to evoke the luminous crystalline appearance of the Holy City, whose "wall was built of jasper, while the city was pure gold, clear as glass" (Rev. 21:18). The Gothic Cathedral, indeed, in its ordered complexity, resembled a city more than it did a temple within a city. Or else it combined the two ideas, like the New Jerusalem itself. It was a microcosmic model of the universe, as befitted the body of God. And its ordering principles included the Pythagorean and Euclidean mathematics that Suger had inherited from the ancient Greeks by way of Boethius and the Arabs. It was in fact the Arabs who had first developed a form of architecture involving pointed arches, and increased contact with the Muslim world during the Crusades led to this style being adopted gradually in the West, replacing the rounded arches of the Romanesque. When Chartres cathedral burned down and had to be rebuilt in 1145, Adelard's translation of Euclid (the major text of ancient Greek geometry, until then completely unknown in the West) was being taught in the schools, and especially in the school of Chartres. Other innovations, such as flying buttresses and large stained glass windows, developed from this.

Of Suger's prototypical Gothic church of Saint-Denis, Schloeder writes: "Here is a church with integrity in its structural elements, perfect proportion in its ruling geometries, and a radiance that activates its material composition."[24] Integrity, radiance, and proportion were the three elements of beauty as defined later by St. Thomas. The concept of "integrity" here refers not merely to a kind of internal coherence, but to

23. On all this, with the relevant quotations from Abbot Suger and Bishop Durandus, see Schloeder 1998, 187–208. Much more detail on the Gothic specifically is provided in Burckhardt 1995, and Mâle 1958, as well as the classic thirteenth-century work by Durandus himself, *The Rationale Divinorum Officiorum*. Hani 2007 provides an impressive synthesis of this tradition.

24. Schloeder 1998, 199.

the kind of perfection a thing attains when it has all it needs to be itself, to perform its authentic function (in this case, to facilitate prayer).

None of this is to say that an authentic church architecture for today will be modeled on the Gothic. According to Rudolf Wittkower, medieval architects tended to build on *geometrical* principles, using circles, squares, triangles, and pentagons, whereas Renaissance architects preferred *arithmetical* principles, epitomized in the simple ratios of the musical scale.[25] Both could appeal to the Pythagorean tradition and the *Timaeus*, but Renaissance architecture attempted to implant musical harmony directly into stone in a way the earlier period did not. As a result, Renaissance architects were less interested in irrationals such as the golden ratio or √2 and √3 (the latter, which featured in the design of the Gothic cathedrals, being the diagonals of a square and cube respectively whose sides are one unit long), preferring the rational numbers of musical harmony.

Wittkower notes the other main differences: the Gothic floorplan echoed the form of Christ's human body on the Cross, and the distance between heaven and earth was expressed in vertical elongation, whereas the Renaissance, influenced by the Greek Cross of Byzantium, preferred the circular form (a square base topped by a dome) as though peering directly at divine perfection. Another shift took place in the Baroque. While the Renaissance had aimed at perfect harmony, the Baroque was a period of agitation and ecstasy. Reflecting the mood of Romanticism, as well as the cosmology of the period, its architects deliberately employed discord to express tension, feeling, and movement everywhere (albeit mystically resolved in the heavenly choirs of angels and representations of the Trinity)—demonstrating "a new *conception of space directed towards infinity*: form is dissolved in favour of the *magic spell of light*."[26]

The traditional principles of harmony in building are not obscure, but they can be applied in many different ways—perhaps in ways not yet imagined. Architects like Christopher Alexander, Duncan G. Stroik, Stephen J. Schloeder, and Daniel Lee are rediscovering the secrets of humane architecture. In architecture as in

25. Wittkower 1998.
26. Wölfflin 1984, 64.

music, we are beginning to appreciate once more the importance of formal beauty.

At Home in the Cosmos

The word "ecology" was coined only as recently as 1873, by the German zoologist Ernst Haeckel. He based it on the Greek word *oikos* meaning "house, dwelling place, habitation" (plus, of course, *logos*). But though the scientific study of ecology, referring to the complex interrelationships of biological entities with each other and with their environment, is a modern development, the traditional worldview has a great deal to say on the matter. The medievals did not possess posters showing the fragile earth floating in a dark sea of space, but the principles underlying the *quadrivium*, even today, can help us learn to dwell more wisely in our common home.

We often talk about the "environmental movement," or about a modern concern for the "environment." It is worth noting that these terms are misleading, since they imply an opposition between humanity (or whichever species is under discussion) and its surroundings, reducing the rest of nature to a kind of backdrop—and at worst to a complex set of raw materials and mechanical forces. The insight that ecologists have come to in the second half of the last century runs counter to this view. It reveals the interdependence of all living things in a world that is more than a mechanism, more than the sum of its parts, perhaps even in some sense alive in its own right. But this is little more than a rediscovery in scientific terms of what had already been understood "poetically" in all previous civilizations. C. S. Lewis, who knew and loved the medieval universe, describes it as "tingling with anthropomorphic life, dancing, ceremonial, a festival not a machine."[27]

The full weight of Lewis's statement will only be felt when we come to the last chapter of this book, but for now the point is that for our preindustrial ancestors the world was not a machine. It was an

27. Cited in Ward 2008, 24. Michael Ward shows that each of Lewis's seven Narnian chronicles was organized around characteristics associated with one of the seven traditional "planets," which he regarded as spiritual symbols of permanent value.

organic whole, ordered from within, animated by a hierarchy of souls, perhaps even by a "world soul." This is not pantheism, although it could become so once the transcendence of God had been forgotten. It meant that nature possessed a sacred and spiritual value, by virtue of its creation by God and the immanent presence of God within it. The world was a book, pregnant with meanings that God had placed there. All things, even the conjectured world soul, were creatures. The stars were angelic creatures, the movements of their high dance helping to determine the pattern of events unfolding below. The elements themselves were conscious beings, according to the sense of analogy, participating in their own way in the cosmic intelligence. Admittedly, St. Francis of Assisi was hardly a typical medieval man, but his ability to address the animals and even the elements in personal terms—easily dismissed by a modern mentality as superstitious nonsense and the "pathetic fallacy"—was the intensified version of an experience that seems to have been commonplace.

> All praise be yours, My Lord, through Brothers Wind and Air,
> And fair and stormy, all the weather's moods,
> By which you cherish all that you have made.
>
> All praise be yours, my Lord, through Sister Water,
> So useful, lowly, precious and pure.
>
> All praise be yours, my Lord, through Brother Fire,
> Through whom you brighten up the night.
> How beautiful is he, how gay! Full of power and strength.
>
> All praise be yours, my Lord, through Sister Earth, our
> mother,
> Who feeds us in her sovereignty, and produces
> Various fruits with colored flowers and herbs.

This extract from the *Canticle of Brother Sun* may be the expression of a new outburst of spiritual feeling for nature, but it is in strictest continuity with many parts of the Christian and Hebrew tradition. The Canticle of Daniel, for example, calls upon all of creation to bless the Lord, including the sun and moon, stars of the heavens, clouds of the sky, showers and rain.[28] For G. K. Chesterton in *St. Francis of Assisi*, the saint was able to attain such pure joy in the things of nature precisely because Christianity had spent the previous millennium trying to purify the world of degenerate forms of paganism that had enslaved man to the living forces of nature, including his own lower nature. Now the natural world could again—in the eyes of a saint—appear as it once was and in its essence always remains, a Garden of Eden. Just as the animals obeyed Adam and permitted him to name them, so the wolf would lay his paw in the hand of Francis, and on one notable occasion a red hot poker would at his request decline to inflict pain on the man who had addressed it with such courtesy.

The animals, plants, and minerals, the stars and elements, were universally thought to "praise" their maker, either simply by their very existence, or when called upon to do so by man (who gives them a voice they do not possess in themselves). Man, as a microcosm containing in himself all the elements of nature and faculties or powers corresponding to both animals and angels, occupied a central place in the universe. It was because of his ontological importance in the order of being that medieval astronomers placed him at the center.[29] They understood—and the earlier church fathers may have understood even better—that Adam's role in the cosmos was a priestly and mediatory one from the beginning. That role had been restored in Christ, who by assuming human nature had in a way assumed *the whole of nature* by taking on a body.

They may not have had (or needed) the term "ecology," but the ancient writers were deeply aware of the interrelatedness of the natural world, and of man as the focus or nexus of that world, which they expressed in the doctrine of correspondences. It was, of course, more poetic than scientific in its formulation, but it expressed a profound insight that remains valid, and the present ecological crisis could only have developed in a world that has forgotten it, or forgotten to live by it. The fundamental human act is prayer, which is the remembrance and

28. Dan. 3:57–88, 56.

29. Modern thought tends to regard man as nothing more than an animal, but implicitly admits his centrality by making him solely responsible for the destruction of the biosphere.

invocation of God (as Simone Weil would say, prayer is "attention").[30] This act is that by which heaven and earth are linked together, and most religious traditions of mankind would agree that it is what keeps the world in existence—it is only when the last person ceases to remember God that the end will come. The harmony of creation depends upon it: once the created world is no longer "attuned" by our prayer to the heavenly harmonies that transcend hearing, only chaos can follow, and the war of one element against another. The Wisdom of Solomon is full of such admonitions. "For creation, serving thee who hast made it, exerts itself to punish the unrighteous, and in kindness relaxes on behalf of those who trust in thee" (Wis. 16:24).[31]

One implication from the doctrine that man is a microcosm, a "little world," is that the disorder in the macrocosm is *our fault*, being a reflection or projection of our own interior dis-ease. When Adam fell from grace, the whole creation was somehow dis-graced, or put out of joint. The healing of the world therefore cannot be envisaged without a reordering and a healing of the inner world of imagination, intelligence, and will. This intuition is easy to relate to the modern study of ecology and to the broader development of a more holistic worldview in postmodern science. As such it also provides a point of entry for understanding the tradition of virtue ethics. It is hard to develop an adequate moral theory based on rights alone that can address the need to conserve natural resources and biodiversity—although attempts have been made to formulate rights for animals and for future generations. It is easier for the average person to think in terms of the need to act virtuously, both with regard to animals and with regard to our use of material things. The damage we wreak in the world is much more obviously the result of cruelty, greed, selfishness, and impatience than it is the violation of some implicit legal code of rights. By putting the emphasis back on our own integrity,

30. The Catholic Mass or Orthodox Divine Liturgy is the highest form of such invocation, *anamnesis*, and mediation.

31. Pico della Mirandola, who summed so much of the Christian-Pythagorean tradition in the late fifteenth century, writes along these lines: "It is reasonable that to the same extent that we do injury not only to ourselves but to the universe, which we encompass within us, and to almighty God, the creator of the world itself, we should also experience all things in the world as the most severe punishers and powerful avengers of injuries, with God among the foremost" (Pico 1965, 136).

and on the cardinal virtues of prudence, justice, temperance, and fortitude, we are laying the foundation for a way of life that would be truly sustainable over time.[32]

It is easy to romanticize past ages as times of ecological harmony simply because they did not possess the technology to do the kind of harm we inflict so easily. Human nature was the same then as now, and was certainly not unfallen in the Middle Ages. Nevertheless, there is an objective difference between a way of life limited in the damage it can inflict on creation, and a way of life founded on the unlimited aspiration to consume and enjoy, one also equipped with the means to change the planet in unpredictable ways. The stability of a preindustrial economy is one thing; our task is to achieve a similar stability in a postindustrial age, and the challenge may seem impossible. We can start by recognizing in our own hearts the tendencies that lead to greed, injustice, and destruction. Then we must seek to ensure these tendencies do not determine our technology and our economy.

Secrets of the Sky

As we have seen, observance of the laws of harmony has been traditionally believed to attune the soul to a heavenly ideal. The spheres associated with the planets, representing levels of the universe or the elements in its construction, were thought to be moved by angels. Each sang a certain note, together expressing the harmony of the

32. For a detailed survey of the metaphysical and historical roots of the ecological crisis see Nasr 1996. This book by a Muslim scholar extends the analysis already found in his groundbreaking early work, *The Encounter of Man and Nature*, which was based on lectures given as early as 1966. Christian treatments of the roots of the crisis have taken awhile to catch up, although Romano Guardini's *Letters from Lake Como*, written in the 1920s, already goes to the heart of the matter, and the writings of E. F. Schumacher in the 1970s made an important contribution. Paulos Mar Gregorios worked out an ecological theology in the tradition of Gregory of Nyssa and Maximus the Confessor for the World Council of Churches in 1987, published as *The Human Presence*. Catholic teaching on ecological responsibility was summarized in *The Compendium of the Social Doctrine of the Church* (Vatican, 2004), and by Cahal B. Daly in *The Minding of Planet Earth* in the same year.

universe; a harmony that may be transmitted through music to the human soul.

The idea was famously expressed by Lorenzo, a character in Shakespeare's *Merchant of Venice*, gazing up at the starry sky from the garden of Belmont, a villa near Venice:

> Look how the floor of Heaven
> Is thick inlaid with patines of bright gold
> There's not the smallest orb that thou beholdest
> But in his motion like an angel sings
> Still quiring to the young-eyed cherubims
> Such harmony is in immortal souls.
> But, while this muddy vesture of decay
> Doth grossly close it in, we cannot hear it.[33]

According to C. S. Lewis, the music of the spheres

> is the only sound which has never for one split second ceased in any part of the universe; with this positive we have no negative to contrast. Presumably if (*per impossibile*) it ever did stop, then with terror and dismay, with a dislocation of our whole auditory life, we should feel that the bottom had dropped out of our lives. But it never does. The music which is too familiar to be heard enfolds us day and night and in all ages.[34]

The last great attempt to discover the ultimate secret of the universe in a grand synthesis of geometry, music, astrology, and astronomy was Johannes Kepler's *Harmonices Mundi* ("The Harmonies of the World"), published in 1618. The history of this achievement is enormously instructive. Kepler (d. 1630), like his predecessor Copernicus, was a fervent Pythagorean, and it was a belief in the causal role of perfect geometrical and numerical forms in nature that drove his intellectual quest.

> Why waste words? Geometry existed before the Creation, is co-eternal with the mind of God, *is God himself* (what exists in God that is not God himself?); geometry provided God with a model for the Creation

33. *The Merchant of Venice*, act 5, scene 1.
34. Cited in Ward 2008, 21.

> and was implanted into man, together with God's own likeness—and not merely conveyed to his mind through the eyes.[35]

The hypothesis of a sun-centered planetary system, as opposed to an earth-centered one, was developed not because it could explain the observed facts more accurately (for at first it could not) but for aesthetic and symbolic reasons. But it was Kepler's Christianity, in combination with his Pythagorean enthusiasm, that made possible the birth of modern science.[36] The problem with the traditional method of relating everything to the simple mathematical archetypes of Pythagorean numerology and harmony is that if you *start* with the archetypes and try to deduce the forms and movements of the universe you will almost certainly go wrong—and you will end up having to bend the facts to reconcile them with your empirical observations. The traditional method is not pragmatic, after all, but contemplative. It is not oriented toward the practical. Science in the modern sense was born when Kepler began to give the same weight to empirical observation as to his theoretical concerns, and that was related to his conviction that a benign Creator was responsible for the way the world worked, on earth as well as in heaven.

If, as many of the ancients believed, the material and changeable world is merely an imperfect shadow of the unchanging eternal, we can hardly hope to find matter conforming perfectly to mathematical laws. So it was that by Kepler's time it was accepted that mathematical devices (such as epicycles) could be used by astronomers to predict the movements of the heavens, without anyone really believing that they existed in reality. Astronomy was not concerned with finding physical explanations for things. After all, what cause is needed, other than God? Astronomers were concerned exclusively with "saving the appearances" by finding accurate ways

35. Kepler, cited in Koestler 1989, 264. Koestler's Kepler is an attractive if bumbling character—he describes himself as a "foolish bird." I particularly identify with his "peculiar kind of memory which makes him promptly forget everything he is not interested in, but which is quite wonderful in relating one idea to another" (243).

36. It was Isaac Newton who later found the hidden connections between these three laws of planetary motion, in the form of his theory of gravity. For example, the first law—that the planetary orbits are ellipses—is due to the inverse square law relating force to distance.

of analyzing heavenly movements into their component circles—that is, devising mathematical descriptions of these appearances using perfect circles without assuming any physical explanation of them whatever.[37]

Kepler's breakthrough came because he introduced a "why?" question where the astronomers of his day didn't see the need for one. He sought physical causes for heavenly motions. And that was not because he believed less in God as the cause of everything, but because he had more respect for the physical world as God's creation and as the image of God's mind. It was the first step toward Newton's cosmos, in which the same universal laws (such as gravity) governed both the earth and the heavens.

Take the orbits of the planets, for example. At the age of twenty-five Kepler thought he had discovered that the orbits of the six visible planets orbiting the sun (Mercury, Venus, Earth, Mars, Jupiter, Saturn) fit beautifully within the five Platonic solids, arranged one inside another. This would explain why there are precisely six, and not more, and why they orbit where they do. Of course, we now know there are more planets than those visible to the naked eye. Koestler calls this a classic example of "false inspiration" that nevertheless triggered a series of breakthroughs that proved to be of lasting importance.

Unfortunately for Kepler's peace of mind, the fit between the orbits and the Platonic solids proved to be inexact, according to the data he had taken from Copernicus. His continuing unease with these discrepancies drove him to seek out the much more accurate observations of Tycho Brahe, whom he met early in the year 1600. Out of this meeting of two great astronomers eventually came Kepler's *New Astronomy*, his physics of the sky, in 1609. In that book he reports his discovery that the planets move around the sun not in the perfect circles that seemed most appropriate to celestial bodies, but in ellipses. At one point he compared this to finding a "load of dung" in the heavens.

37. There may have been more to Kepler's poetic intuitions (what Koestler calls his "Baroque fantasies" and Burtt calls "crude inherited superstitions") than conventional wisdom allows. John Martineau and Richard Heath have recently shown that Kepler's intuition about the relations of the planetary orbits to the Platonic solids were not so far off the mark after all (see www.woodenbooks.com).

Pure deduction from an aesthetic ideal had gone astray, but careful observation and measurement had led to a correct conclusion seemingly at odds with traditional cosmology.

The irony is that if we contemplate the *result* of this observation, we find that an unexpected beauty reveals itself. For the medieval astronomers were wrong: there is actually nothing imperfect about an ellipse. It differs from a circle by having two centers or foci rather than one (the sun occupying one of them), so that the sum of the distances from any point on the circumference to the two centers remains constant. Thus the planetary orbit is determined by two centers, the visible and the invisible, just as the life of any creature must revolve around the incarnate Logos and the invisible Father. What could be more elegant? Or as Kepler came to see, if the circle represents "transcendental" perfection, and the straight line represents the created world, an ellipse (as the combination of the two) represents perfectly the incarnation of the ideal in the created order. Kepler's original mistake did not lie in his Christian Pythagoreanism, but in his attempt to prejudge the mathematical forms he would find in nature. He should have been happy to be led by observation, confident that what he discovered would (eventually) turn out to have appropriate symbolic properties.

In order to make Pythagorean sense out of these strange elliptical movements in the sky, Kepler tried to reconcile the orbits of the planets with the classical harmonic proportions. He eventually found the correspondence he was looking for in the variations of the *angular velocities* of the planets as seen from the sun, by comparing the speed at which they were traveling at different parts of their orbits. This is an example of the right way of doing things: to look at what really happens, and discover the beauty in it.

Kepler had now discovered the first two of his immortal "three laws" of planetary motion. The third came to him as he tried to find the relationship between a planet's period around the sun and its distance. Kepler thought there had to be a connection, if the sun was indeed master of the solar system. It turned out that the *square* of the period is proportional to the *cube* of the mean distance. Not intuitively obvious, but beautiful nonetheless.

As Koestler tells Kepler's story, the harmonies he searched for and eventually found were psychologically but not otherwise particularly significant. They lured him onward, but the more important Pythagorean insight that he had revived after a millennium and a half of neglect was simply that mathematical relations hold the secret of the universe—the *whole* universe, above and below the moon—and need to be uncovered by precise empirical observation.

The Ptolemaic astronomers, assuming circular motion with the earth stationary at the center, had tried to account for the retrogression of the planets against the stars by means of a complex pattern of epicycles and deferents—wheels within wheels. We do not have to revert to their geocentric description to appreciate simple patterns that reveal themselves in the relative motion of the planets, as they pursue their separate eccentric paths around the sun, each at a different speed. Not only are the periods of the planets related to each other in fairly precise harmonic proportions (2:5 in the case of Jupiter and Saturn, for example, and 1:Φ in the case of Earth and Venus), but each traces a lovely sequence of loops around the other that reveal aspects of their geometrical relationship. Venus and Earth produce a particularly beautiful five-petaled "flower" containing a pentagram of close conjunctions over 8 years (13 Venusian years).

Thus the solar system as understood and measured by modern astronomers abounds with beauty that would warm the heart of any Christian Pythagorean. One final example: ancient and medieval geometers were tantalized by the problem of "squaring the circle," which meant finding the square whose perimeter (or alternatively area) measured exactly the same as that of a given circle. It is one of the strange coincidences in which the solar system abounds that the problem is "solved" by the respective sizes of the earth and the moon, which are in the ratio of 11:3. Thus if the moon were rolled around the earth's surface, its center would describe a circle equal to the perimeter of a square inscribed around the earth (31,680 miles).[38]

The harmonics of the planetary orbits are well known. Something analogous must surely apply within the subatomic world (quantum harmonics?), since all energy is a kind of vibration. These different levels of creation—the macro- and the micro-world, with humanity between—are

38. For more on all this, see Martineau 2006 and Schneider 2006.

bound up in a single whole. It has often been remarked that if any of the main physical constants (such as one of the four fundamental forces of nature, Planck's constant, or the speed of light) had been slightly different than they are, the universe could not have developed into a suitable habitation for life. In this sense too the cosmos is a beautifully ordered whole, precisely tuned to permit human existence.[39]

Everywhere we look in nature, we tend to find structure or form. The planets occupy distinct orbits, rotating in close numerical relation to one another. Materials vibrate at certain frequencies that harmonize together. Electrons fall into distinct "shells" around the nucleus of the atom, jumping from one level to another depending on the units of energy they acquire. In evolutionary biology, creatures do not appear randomly across the whole range of physical possibility, but fall into families and species each of which expresses a particular type of creaturehood. All these distinct forms we observe in the universe indicate what Pope Benedict calls the "inner design of its fabric."[40] They can be read as approximations to the fundamental "ideas" that lie behind the creation. Thus even today the concept of harmony developed by the Pythagoreans can help us understand the way the unity and diversity of the world unfolds.

The End of the Road

Music, architecture, astronomy, and physics—the physical arts and their applications—demonstrate the fundamental intuition behind the Liberal Arts tradition of education, which is that the world is an ordered whole, a "cosmos," whose beauty becomes more apparent the more carefully and deeply we study it. By preparing ourselves

39. The so-called "anthropic principle." Some scientists attempt to escape the obvious implications by positing the existence of multiple domains or universes, making it entirely natural that we would find ourselves in the one that happens to support human life. This is a pretty desperate move. By the way, an extension of the anthropic principle would state that the world's physical structure is the way it is not only in order to support human life, but *to communicate metaphysical truths to us symbolically*. In other words we are justified in reading something into the symbolism of the sun "rising" and "setting," even if we know that it is the earth that moves around the sun.

40. Ratzinger 1995a, 26.

in this way to contemplate the higher mysteries of philosophy and theology, we become more alive, more fully human. This beautiful order can be studied at every level and in every context, from the patterns made by cloud formation or river erosion to that of the leaves around the stem of the most obnoxious weed, from the shape of the human face as it catches the light, or the way keys are ordered in a concerto by Bach, to the collision of stellar nebulae and particles in an atomic furnace.

Yet at the same time, while studying and appreciating the intuitions that lay behind the cosmological sciences of the *quadrivium*, we cannot today simply revert to the worldview of the Middle Ages. The ancient mathematical theories of music and astronomy contain elements we need to retrieve, but they were not themselves entirely adequate. In his theological study of Western tonal music, Jeremy Begbie asks, in the Great Tradition stemming from Pythagoras,

> Is the created world being treated as able to glorify God *in its own way*, by virtue of its own distinctive patterns, rhythms, and movements? Many have argued that the streams of thought that guided much medieval thinking about music did not pay enough attention to the distinctive order and harmony of the universe as it is and as it could be. Out of a keenness to assume direct and necessary correspondences between the created world and God, to preserve (in some cases) a "hierarchy of being," it is debateable whether the structures of creation were always being respected in their full integrity and potential.[41]

We have seen that question arise in connection with astronomy too. Yet in noting the shift in our modern thinking "*from the cosmological to the anthropological*, from justifying music in terms of the cosmos at large to justifying it solely in terms of human needs and aspirations"[42] (and for all his slight suspicion of the influence of "Platonic" otherworldliness on the arts), Begbie wonders if something immensely valuable has been lost along the way.

41. Begbie 2008, 92–93.
42. Ibid., 94.

> For all that we might smile benignly at in the mathematical clumsiness and rhetorical hyperbole of the classical philosopher of music or the intellectual abstractions and tetchy fussiness of the medieval theorist, is there not something in the notion of being "cradled" in God's created *harmonia* that is worth recovering?[43]

In late 2007, the themes I have been discussing in this book hit the headlines all over the world when a maverick physicist, Garrett Lisi, published online a paper entitled "An Exceptionally Simple Theory of Everything."[44] In it, he suggested all known subatomic particles and forces (and a few unknown ones, which he predicted would be found by the Large Hadron Collider in Switzerland) could be located on a matrix provided by E8, an eight-dimensional shape discovered in 1887 that is regarded as the most elegant and intricate example of mathematical symmetry. As Lisi put it in the online paper, he had devised "a comprehensive unification program, describing all fields of the standard model and gravity as parts of a uniquely beautiful mathematical structure. The principal bundle connection and its curvature describe how the E8 manifold twists and turns over spacetime, reproducing all known fields and dynamics through pure geometry."

The theory was incomplete, and the predictions still to be tested, but what makes this interesting is the philosophy of science that lies behind it. "We exist in a universe described by mathematics," wrote Lisi. "But which math? Although it is interesting to consider that the universe may be the physical instantiation of all mathematics, there is a classic principle for restricting the possibilities: The mathematics of the universe should be beautiful. A successful description of nature should be a concise, elegant, unified mathematical structure consistent with experience."

43. Ibid., 95. On the previous page he quotes Daniel Chua's striking comment, "The harmony of the spheres has collapsed into the song of the self." He concludes that the "broad intuition" and "persistent concern" of the Great Tradition, "to construe the making and hearing of musical sounds as grounded in divinely bestowed matrices of order," is "surely correct and not to be sacrificed thoughtlessly" (233–34).

44. http://arxiv.org/PS_cache/arxiv/pdf/0711/0711.0770v1.pdf

Lisi's particular theory failed, but the drive of science is in this direction. Others will try, guided by the same intuition that *the truth is beautiful*, the same compulsion to discover *the truth in beauty*. But as Stephen M. Barr has pointed out, if science can explain the design of the world by discovering a deeper and simpler design among the laws of nature, it still "has no way to explain the ultimate design of nature."[45] Armed with a convincing Theory of Everything, it will have reached the end of the road of science. But the end of the road is the beginning of another and wider landscape. Science can discover the laws of nature, but not why they are that way, nor why there is anything to obey them. That is why cosmology leads only to the threshold of theology.

45. Barr 2003, 106. See also the work of the 2008 Templeton prizewinner, the distinguished priest-physicist Michael Heller, on the mystery of the world's comprehensibility in "Chaos, Probability, and the Comprehensibility of the World," available online at www.templetonprize.org. Heller's statement at the Templeton news conference on March 12, 2008 (available on the same site) summarizes some of his significant insights. To ask about the cause of the universe is not to ask for "a cause like all other causes" but "the root of all possible causes," and therefore "a cause of mathematical laws." Contrary to the exponents of evolution by "Intelligent Design," he argues, *chance* should not be considered a rival to *design*. "Chance and random processes are elements of the mathematical blueprint of the universe in the same way as other aspects of the world architecture." Both are woven together in the symphony of creation. "Elements of necessity determine the pattern of possibilities and dynamical paths of becoming, but they leave enough room for chancy events to make this becoming rich and individual." In a striking phrase, he speaks of the greatest mystery of all being the "entanglement of the Human Mind with the Mind of God."

6

The Liturgical Consummation of Cosmology

The sciences become hyper-materialist and reductive when they are severed from their theological ground, and the arts, when celebrated for their own sake, apart from a theological purpose, become morbid, sentimental, or bizarre; even abstract mathematics devolves into a fussy and self-preoccupied rationalism when its link to sacred geometry is lost.

Robert Barron[1]

I have suggested several times in this book that the modern era can be characterized by a certain outlook shaped, in part, by the overthrow or displacement of ancient metaphysics. We call this outlook "secular," and it may take the extreme form of materialism, though it may also take religious forms. As David L. Schindler has argued in *Heart of the World, Center of the Church*, even the protection of religion often takes the form of its privatization, with faith

1. Barron 2007, 156.

being progressively excluded from any real influence over public life, morality, and technology.

The outlook that was overthrown was based on what the Middle Ages termed "realism"—not in the modern senses of being "down to earth" or "accurate," but meaning that ideas such as *just*, *beautiful*, *cat*, or *five*, which can be used to describe many different things in the world, possess a reality of their own distinct from that of the individuals or acts they qualify. What displaced this view, starting with thinkers such as Abelard and William of Ockham—the *via moderna* mentioned in an earlier chapter—was philosophical "nominalism." It held that the world consists only of particular individual things, which we need to describe and to which we therefore attach labels. Ideas are simply our way of organizing groups of individual things: they are the labels we choose, for our own purposes, to stick on to bits of reality.

Another relevant sense of "realism" is that the real world (whether made up exclusively of individual things or not) is ontologically independent of our own thoughts and experience of it. This sense of realism survived the assault of nominalism, but was attacked again by the idealism of Kant and Hegel. It is notable that both senses are opposed by the Copenhagen interpretation of quantum mechanics, at least in the popular understanding. A well-known paraphrase of Niels Bohr's view runs as follows: "There is no quantum world. There is only an abstract physical description. It is wrong to think that the task of physics is to find out how nature is. Physics concerns what we can say about nature." Furthermore, this interpretation seems to make reality (for example, the state of an electron) dependent on an act of observation. Einstein was never able to accept it for that reason, while David Bohm and others have proposed alternative "realist" interpretations of the same experimental observations. It seems that modern physics does not necessarily contradict common sense or ancient metaphysics after all. (We have already seen how Bohr and Heisenberg felt able to cite Plato and Pythagoras, and their opponents are even more entitled to do so.)[2]

2. There have been numerous attempts to reconnect quantum mechanics with ancient metaphysics. Cf. Caldecott 1998. For Simone Weil they all start at the wrong place: classical physics was at a dead end, but modern physics lost touch with reality

The Construction of Modernity

The point here is simply that we are living in an era shaped by philosophical battles that most of us are unaware ever took place. The victors wrote the history books, of course, to make the outcome look inevitable. Let me try to connect all this with the "secularism" that currently has the world's intellectual elites under its spell.

Writers such as Louis Dupré, Charles Taylor, Robert Barron, and Catherine Pickstock confirm that nominalism, or the philosophical voluntarism associated with it, lies behind secular modernity.[3] The story these writers tell (setting aside various differences in emphasis) is of a philosophical shift, associated not only with a severing of the intimate bond between cosmology and ethics, facts and values, but with a changing sense of the self, and of the relation between self and society. This shift was also the beginning of modern individualism, and of the subjective turn that led to what Taylor in *A Secular Age* calls a "buffered self" in a "disenchanted world." The modern person feels himself to be disengaged from the world around him, rather than intrinsically related to it (by family, tribe, birthplace, vocation, and so forth). He is expected to forge his own destiny by an exercise of choice. He is concerned less with what is right than with what his

---

at the moment it invented the notion of the "quantum," making energy discontinuous when it must by its nature be continuous: "Planck's formula, composed of a constant whose source one cannot imagine and a number which corresponds to a probability, has no relation to any thought" (1968, 23). She did not dispute that the calculations worked; what she objected to was abandoning the attempt to understand *why* they worked. Cf. Morgan 2005, 53–58.

3. See Bibliography. Voluntarism is sometimes traced back to the scholastic philosopher Duns Scotus. Benedict XVI in his talk at Regensburg in September 2006 describes Scotus's voluntarism as potentially leading to an "image of a capricious God, who is not even bound to truth and goodness." Pickstock and Barron blame Scotus's univocal concept of existence, i.e., his placing of God and the creature in the same category of being. Previously the being of God—the sense in which he "exists"—was only analogously related to the being of creatures, but henceforth "God and creatures are appreciated as existing side by side, as beings of varying types and degrees of intensity. Furthermore, unanchored from their shared participation in God, no longer grounded in a common source, creatures lose their essential connectedness to one another. Isolated and self-contained individuals (God the supreme being and the many creatures) are now what is most basically real" (Barron 2007, 14). For Pickstock it is a small jump from there to Descartes and the "necrophilia" of the present age: the embrace of atomized, mechanized nature.

rights are, or rather he grounds the former on the latter. The world for him is just a neutral space for his action, his free choice, and the greatest mysteries lie not outside but within himself.

Many puzzling features of the modern world can be understood in this way. With no hierarchy of ordered forms to draw upon (since the existence of such forms had been denied by nominalism), God's rule over the universe became "free" in the sense of arbitrary, or whimsical: the new image of God was of an absolute, albeit usually benign, dictator. His grand design for the universe was one of "interlocking causes, not harmonized meanings,"[4] and as the concept of efficient causality absorbed that of formal causality in the old scheme of things, human as well as divine actions had to be justified as "efficient": part of a process of *exchange for anticipated benefit*, as payment for specific desired outcomes. The concept of a "final" cause (goal) or *telos* was secularized. This is how the whole world became one gigantic market. Finally, if the only Forms are those we invent, the social and political order has to be created by the imposition of will—at first by God, then by a divinely appointed king, and (after the overthrow of the *ancient régime*) by individual choices made at the ballot box—or by those capable of manipulating those choices, by means subtle or crude.

In hindsight we can see that this philosophical shift also prepared the ground for the Reformation, which emphasized individual conscience and pared away the fabric of traditions and "sacramentals" by which the self had been embedded in a social cosmos. But without those ties, without that embeddedness, nature was drained of grace, and our connection to the transcendent God became less a matter of imagination or intellect or feeling than of sheer willpower. All that was needed was for us to stop willing it, and it would cease to be, which is what effectively happened in the later stages of the Enlightenment.

This all-pervasive modern mentality is what we are up against, in education as everywhere else. So the question is now, what can be done about it, if anything? The Enlightenment is not something you can simply unthink. So how are we to combat the negative effects of individualism, without losing the benefits of self-consciousness and rationality?

4. Taylor 2007, 177.

The key lies, I believe, with revelation and worship. What defines secularism more than anything is an *inability to pray*, and the modern world in its worst aspects is a systematic assault on the very idea of worship, an idea that begins with the acknowledgment of a Transcendent that reveals itself in the Immanent. Balthasar was right: once lose the sense of objective beauty, of the Forms in the fabric of the world (confirmed and strengthened by revelation), and eventually the ability to pray goes too. The fully "buffered" self that has no Forms to contemplate in the cosmos, no reality higher than itself, has no God to turn to.

Prayer is a vital dimension of fully human living. But while we can all pray on our own, it is always in some sense a community thing. It turns us away from ourselves toward God, and in so doing it turns us toward each other (or should do). In fact human civilization has always been built around an act of worship, a public liturgy. Liturgy (from the Greek *leitourgia*: public work or duty) technically means any kind of religious service done on behalf of a community. Liturgical prayer is a way of being in tune with our society, with other people. But if we are to renew our civilization by renewing our worship, we must understand also that liturgy is a way of being in tune with the motions of the stars, the dance of atomic particles, and the harmony of the heavens that resembles a great song. And Catholic liturgy takes us even deeper than that. It takes us to the source of the cosmos itself, into the sacred precincts of the Holy Trinity where all things begin and end (whether they know it or not), and to the source of all artistic and scientific inspiration, of all *culture*.

> For in him all the fulness of God was pleased to dwell, and through him to reconcile to himself all things, whether on earth or in heaven, making peace by the blood of his cross. (Col. 1:19–20)

Liturgy, therefore, is not something that is confined to the services taking place in a church building. As we saw in a previous chapter, creation, through its very being, gives a kind of liturgical praise to God. Eric Peterson sums this up as follows:

> The . . . worship of the Church is not the liturgy of a human religious society, connected with a particular temple, but worship which pervades the whole universe and in which sun, moon and all the stars take part.

> And so we read in the introduction to the *Sanctus* of the *Liturgy of St. James*: "Him do praise the heavens and the heaven of heavens and their concerted might, sun and moon and all the singing galaxies of stars, earth, sea and all that they contain."[5]

In discerning how to harmonize his liturgical activity to that of heaven, man takes his cue, as it were, from the cosmos.

Can we see liturgy itself, then, as the "lost key" to humane education that we have been searching for in this book; that is, to the reintegration of all things, all subjects, in a vision of sacred order? Would a renewed appreciation of liturgy help to anchor theories about number and symbolism and quality more profoundly in real life, enabling us to introduce some much needed harmony into our own souls too?

A Sense of the Sacred

We need first to establish a clearer sense of the sacred and its meaning, which (for the reasons outlined above) can hardly be taken for granted. It will help to look at this concept not just in the context of Christianity and Judaism, but in relation to religious experience in general. In 1957, Mircea Eliade wrote an influential book called *Sacred and Profane*. Building on the work of Rudolf Otto, he starts by describing the fundamental religious experience as an encounter with an awe-inspiring mystery (*mysterium tremendum et fascinans*), the "wholly other," the *numen* or divine power. In the face of this Other, the human being "senses his profound nothingness." This experience is as fundamental to human beings as terror, laughter, love, and the sense of beauty, but, though it is practically universal, there are some people who are more liable to it than others, and some societies where it is encouraged more than others. Eliade's book is about the many ways the "sacred" is held to reveal itself.

According to Eliade, a sacred object or place is one that, while belonging to this perceptible world, is set apart in order to manifest something of a wholly different order.

5. Peterson 1964, 22.

> By manifesting the sacred, an object becomes *something else*, yet it continues to remain *itself*, for it continues to participate in its surrounding cosmic milieu. A *sacred* stone remains a *stone*; apparently (or, more precisely, from a profane point of view), nothing distinguishes it from all other stones. But for those to whom a stone reveals itself as sacred, its immediate reality is transformed into a supernatural reality. In other words, for those who have a religious experience all nature is capable of revealing itself as a cosmic sacrality. The cosmos as a whole can become a hierophany [a revelation of sacred order].[6]

Eliade therefore contrasts two ways of being in the world, the sacred and the profane. Traditional or religious man lives in a world permeated and determined by the sense of the sacred—which tends to be equated with being, with reality, and with ultimate creative power. The world we see around us contains objects and places that are sacred in this sense, though not all equally so. Proximity to or representation of the divine determines the graduated structure of the world, with the central point being an axis that connects all-that-is with its origin. Space is not homogeneous (the same in all directions), for the sacred has irrupted within it, revealing the presence of an absolute reality. This manifestation of the *truly real* is the foundation of the world's being, and every sacred mountain, tree, shrine, or holy object contains a reference to it. A people or tribe establishes its place in the universe by finding or being given a central place of this sort and orienting its life around it. Even a house becomes a "home" only by situating itself as a symbolic representation of the world in miniature, complete with an opening (upward or inward) toward the divine. I am thinking of the fireplace, the hearth, or the place where food is cooked, and the chimney through which smoke rises to heaven. Traditionally, it was the fire that symbolized the heart of the home. (We might reflect on what it means that today the TV or computer screen has replaced it.)

The same principles, of course, apply to time as to space. For Christians, the structuring of time—the seven days of the week, the months of the year, the feast days, Easter and Christmas—serves as a way to reconnect us with the transcendent, reminding us of our origin and end. Each cycle leads us back to the alpha, and brings us

6. Eliade 1959, 12.

closer to the omega, by connecting us with the center of time. The season of Advent enables us to share in the pregnant Mary's state of expectation leading up to the world's first sight of the God-Child, and Lent to spend forty days with Jesus in the wilderness doing battle with the devil—even though the events themselves took place long centuries ago "by the clock." (On a personal note, I always feel when in church, especially in Mass, it would be wrong to look at my watch. That is because in a sacred space we are also to some extent in sacred time. For the same reason it would be a kind of desecration to place a clock over the altar.)

Profane man, on the other hand, lives or tries to live in a *desacralized* cosmos (or as Taylor says, a disenchanted one), a world of homogeneous geometrical space and undifferentiated time in which no one place or occasion is more special, more holy, than any other. We fail, of course. We all have birthdays, anniversaries, images, and places that are especially dear to us, which help us define and remember who we are. We build ourselves a nest in the world, staking our claim and building an environment where we feel at home. We all tell ourselves stories that make some sense of our lives. These interior narratives may be harmful or helpful, but they are told over and over again in a silent monologue that "fixes" us as members of a world that has a particular shape, that is familiar and to some extent predictable. (It can be an important part of therapy to bring harmful aspects of this narrative to light and alter them in some significant respect.) We are never pure thinking machines; we feel, remember, and imagine. The difference is that profane man possesses a philosophy which does not allow him to connect these central experiences of life to some transcendent realm, and to the origin of all things.

Desacralized man, Eliade suggests, is the result of a "second Fall" in which even the *memory* of Eden is lost. Whether such an existence can be sustained for long has yet to be discovered. Historically, it is a rather recent phenomenon, dating back less than a hundred years, even if as we have seen its roots lie in the fourteenth century or earlier. All other civilizations known to us have had a strong religious orientation. And no civilization has survived a failure to transmit that orientation through some process of education, initiating a new generation into its vision of cosmic order.

Liturgy as Remembering to Give

A religious society orients itself toward God by having first a cosmogony or a creation story, second an eschatology, a doctrine of the "last things," of the endings of life and time, and thirdly a liturgy—that is, a set of rituals and a way of organizing time and space that situates us in relation to the beginning and end of things (*in via* or in process from one to the other). But, of course, we live in a diverse and pluralistic society, as well as a largely secular one. Is liturgy of relevance to any but a very small group of the self-consciously pious? In order to see why it is, we need to remember that the essence or starting point of liturgy is a very simple one.

Religious service is essentially a work of praise, of giving glory to God. Though it is communal work, and in a sense it helps to *create* community, it is derived from the primordial action of the individual human being, an action more basic to us—when we are authentically ourselves—than even eating or drinking or sleeping; namely, *giving thanks*. For prior to everything else we may do, and whether or not we think of ourselves as "religious," we exist, and liturgy begins by acknowledging that fact with gratitude.

G. K. Chesterton sums it up in his book *Chaucer*:

> There is at the back of all our lives an abyss of light, more blinding and unfathomable than any abyss of darkness; and it is the abyss of actuality, of existence, of the fact that things truly are, and that we ourselves are incredibly and sometimes almost incredulously real. It is the fundamental fact of being, as against not being; it is unthinkable, yet we cannot unthink it, though we may sometimes be unthinking about it; unthinking and especially unthinking. For he who has realized this reality knows that it does outweigh, literally to infinity, all lesser regrets or arguments for negation, and that under all our grumblings there is a subconscious substance of gratitude. The light of the positive is the business of the poets, because they see all things in the light of it more than do other men.[7]

Liturgy therefore starts with *remembrance*. We do not make ourselves from nothing. To be here at all is a gift, and a gift (even if we are at

7. Chesterton 1932, 36–37.

times only obscurely aware of the Giver) evokes a natural desire to give something back to someone. We have only what we have received, but included in that gift is the capacity to transform what we now possess into something that is truly our own. Furthermore, the more grateful we are, and the more conscious of the greatness of the One, the source who gave us existence, the more beautiful we will try to make the gift. That is partly why liturgy has always inspired art. As I once heard an art historian say, "The fine arts were born on the altar."[8]

If we consider only a setting where the liturgical spirit is implicit, a setting where, say, there is no common agreement on a religious faith (even on Christianity broadly understood), it is easy to see that there are ways in which the "substance of gratitude" can still be expressed and made present. The elemental courtesies of conventional etiquette and good manners are the vital channels for preserving this spirit in everyday life. Friends naturally express gratitude and respect, but an education that actively cultivates such modes of behavior will begin the process of building a society that is liturgical to its very core, in which the "air" of grace can circulate. Harmony of soul can only be restored through effort, and the restoration of manners and kindness is an important beginning. Without it, little else is possible.

An Education in Beauty

In a religious setting, of course, the liturgical spirit can be explicit. The giving of thanks is the whole purpose of ritual prayer, the first task of the human being as such. It achieves its highest moment in the act of sacrifice, which is common to every religious tradition. Sacrifice is the offering to God or the gods of a token representing the self or the community. This sacrifice must be continually renewed and repeated according to the rhythms of sacred time by a consecrated official, thus—by means of gift—establishing an exchange or bridge between heaven and earth. In Christianity, where the High Priest and the sacrifice are both the same—Jesus Christ, who is also God—the

8. From art one might go on to apply this "liturgical principle" to the redemption of work, and the ordering of the economy through production, exchange, and consumption, as John Hughes does in his book *The End of Work*, especially chap. 6.

traditional sacrifice is elevated to an inconceivable level.[9] The gifts we bring to the altar are taken up into the sacrifice of Christ on the Cross, so that through the priest we are able to give something to God that is of equal value to (because it is identical with) God's own self-gift.

The liturgy, and at its heart the Mass, is the ultimate *school of thanks*. In the circle of giving, receiving, and being given, the one divine essence is revealed as an eternal threefold liturgy of love, prayer, and praise. When we come to Mass—or to the nearest equivalent of that liturgy our faith permits—we should be able to experience a sense that here, at last, all the threads of our education are being brought together. If we don't, something is wrong with our education or our liturgy. Science and art, mathematics and ethics, history and psychology, the worlds of nature and the spirit, are all present in a liturgy that gives them a home and a meaning.

In *The Crisis of Western Education*, Christopher Dawson identifies the crisis as it applies particularly to our schools, colleges, and universities, in the following terms:

> The result [of modern educational reforms] has been an intellectual anarchy imperfectly controlled by the crude methods of the examination system and of payment by results. The mind of the student is overwhelmed and dazed by the volume of new knowledge which is being accumulated by the labour of specialists, while the necessity for using education as a stepping-stone to a profitable career leaves him little time to stop and think. And the same is true of the teacher, who has become a kind of civil servant tied to a routine over which he can have little control.[10]

As we saw in the first chapter, the solution or remedy he in fact proposes is not to revive the *trivium* and *quadrivium* as such, but to devise a new humanist education with an "intelligible form" based around the historical study of Christian or Western culture.

> What we need is not an encyclopaedic knowledge of all the products of Christian culture, but a study of the culture-process itself from its

9. See the letter to the Hebrews, which is an extended reflection on Jesus as High Priest.

10. Dawson 1989, 119.

> spiritual and theological roots, through its organic historical growth to its cultural fruits. It is this organic relation between theology, history and culture which provides the integrative principle in Catholic higher education, and the only one that is capable of taking the place of the old classical humanism which is disappearing or has already disappeared.[11]

The multiculturalists will naturally object to an exclusive concentration on "Western" culture, but I am sure Dawson is right in this, that the Christian humanists of the future will come from homes and colleges where their own culture has been taught in all its historical depth and with an eye to its intelligible form (which is also ultimately theological, whether we realize it or not). But what I have been suggesting in this book is something more. Dawson's proposal can be expanded. There is more to the *quadrivium* than a mere list of subjects, by now of little historical interest. There is a cosmology. If we look at the underlying principles or ideals that led the ancients to codify the seven Liberal Arts in the first place, we find there a vision in which the arts and sciences, faith and reason, are not separated, as they have been since the Reformation and the Enlightenment in our mainstream philosophies; rather they profoundly complement each other. The key to this vision lies in the notion (traceable back to Pythagoras) of *beauty as cosmic order*, an order that is simultaneously aesthetic, harmonious, symbolic, mathematical, and sacramental. In the present chapter I have argued that the right form of liturgical worship shows us how the universe is ordered from within by the Trinity.

Now of course not all families will share a religious faith, and not all will attend Mass together. Nor should all students even at a Catholic college be obliged to attend Mass, let alone be expected to profess beliefs they do not own. Nevertheless, as Cardinal Ratzinger pointed out before his election as Pope in an essay "On the Essence of the Academy and Its Freedom," there was a reason why Plato set up his Academy in a suburban temple precinct. It had to be under the auspices of a cultic association, in which the Muses were venerated.[12]

11. Ibid., 137–38.
12. Ratzinger 1995b, 40.

The kind of education I am imagining can only take place in an atmosphere of respect toward religion, if not its actual practice.

Today, a person or community or family or college that tries to place the liturgy as a structural principle at the center of things at the very least will convey implicitly to those without a religious faith the presence of an objective order of truth, beauty, goodness, and love—the Logos of all humane education the world over. By keying the year to liturgical time, and punctuating it with feast days, by trying to respect the sanctity of the Sabbath, by encouraging the presence all around us of artistic and architectural symbols that speak of heaven, by preserving the ethos of the Ten Commandments, and by observing nature and learning from tradition, our lives will be patterned after the same principles that govern the universe, and we will be living in a way that suits our own nature and allows it to flourish.

The Holy City

At the end of the book of Revelation, John shows us a holy city descending out of heaven like a bride, a city full of rushing water and wind and the waving branches of trees and the songs of living creatures. This vision of the Church and of the liturgy is also a vision of the cosmos. The Heavenly City is a key to enable the universe itself to be decoded. In it we glimpse the true nature of humanity, and in humanity the purpose and goal of nature. Not that nature only exists to serve fallen man—far from it; but the salvation of man entails the salvation and transformation of the whole cosmic environment in which we live, the animals and plants and minerals, even the colors and numbers and directions that play such an important part in the book of Revelation. These are all reflected in our own being, to which they are inseparably connected, and together with us all these creatures yearn for the coming of the Liturgical City, in which *every tear shall be wiped away* (Rev. 21:4).

The New Jerusalem represents the whole world in its final "saved" form, a giant Ark of living crystal—the universe healed and integrated, a glorious Bride in whom everything of value in the world is rescued and redeemed. It is so intensively unified by liturgy that its citizens share the divine life without needing an external "temple." The city is permeated by the light of God's glory, in which God is seen face to face, a beatifying vision that unites even as it differentiates.

> And I saw no temple in the city, for its temple is the Lord God the Almighty and the Lamb. And the city has no need of sun or moon to shine upon it, for the glory of God is its light, and its lamp is the Lamb. (Rev. 21:22–3)

Everyone becomes more himself or herself in such a city, but (at the same time and for the same reason) more intimately present to every other. In the "Liturgical City" of Revelation there is no Temple, for liturgy itself is transcended. Each discovers his true self, but that self has been found by going outward, by pouring oneself away to help others, by ecstatically appreciating and responding to the face of God revealed in the other person and unveiled in Christ.

Our own earthly cities are not the New Jerusalem, but neither are they the "Babylon" of Revelation 18, the nightmare city of harlots and merchants, heaped high with iniquity and destined to be cast into a burning smoke. Our institutions are a bit of both, for they look in both directions. The "judgment" aspect of Revelation—by which I mean the slaughter and the plagues, the firestorms and earthquakes, the seven bowls of divine wrath, the four horsemen of the apocalypse, the casting into a sea of fire, and all the rest of it—is the measure of the distance from earth to heaven, and the cost of the struggle to bring the one down and the other up to meet in the Marriage of the Lamb. The human task is to build up the Liturgical City by turning our lives back into gift.

Conclusion

Beyond Faith and Reason

> The emptiness and triviality of so much of the rhetoric of official academia is a symptom of a much deeper disorder.
>
> Alasdair MacIntyre[1]

And yet, and yet . . . We are up against so much. Let us retrace our steps slightly and try to see more clearly exactly what we are dealing with.

In *A Secular Age* Charles Taylor contrasts the ancient notion of cosmos with the modern secular universe:

> I use "cosmos" for our forebears' idea of the totality of existence because it contains the idea of an ordered whole. It is not that our own universe isn't in its own way ordered, but in the cosmos the order of

1. MacIntyre 1990, 227. I am quoting him rather out of context. His actual argument is that incommensurable conceptions of rationality in the modern university continually frustrate its inherited Enlightenment aspiration to universal, unified knowledge. The way forward is to find a way to permit rival traditions to challenge each other within the university ("constrained disagreement"), without placing one in a superior position under the false guise of "neutrality"—which of course is what normally happens in our secular age.

> things was a humanly meaningful one. That is, the principle of order in the cosmos was closely related to, often identical with, that which gives shape to our lives.
>
> Thus Aristotle's cosmos has at its apex and centre God, whose ceaseless and unvarying action exemplifies something close to Plato's eternity. But this action, a kind of thinking, is also at the centre of our lives. Theoretical thought is in us that which is "most divine." And for Plato, and this whole mode of thought in general, the cosmos exhibits the order which we should exemplify in our own lives, both individually and as societies.[2]

He adds that for medieval Christians, as for many of the ancients,

> this kind of cosmos is a hierarchy; it has higher and lower levels of being. And it reaches its apex in eternity; it is, indeed, held together by what exists on the level of eternity, the Ideas, or God, or both together—Ideas as the thoughts of the creator.

As Taylor, a Catholic philosopher, knows very well, this is the cosmos that most religious believers still inhabit. Partly he is putting himself in the shoes of those to whom this world is alien, and asking how so many have come to see it that way (his account takes in Renaissance humanism, the Scientific Revolution, the Protestant and Catholic movement of Reform, the birth of the police state, the Enlightenment, the Age of Mobilization, and the Age of Authenticity). Modern people who see the religious cosmos as alien, inhabit not a cosmos but a "universe." A universe, he says,

> has its own kind of order, that exhibited in exceptionless natural laws. But it is no longer a hierarchy of being, and it doesn't obviously point to eternity as the locus of its principle of cohesion. The universe flows on in secular time. Above all, its principles of order are not related to human meaning, at any rate not immediately or evidently.[3]

2. Taylor 2007, 60.

3. Ibid. In vol. 5 of *The Glory of the Lord*, Hans Urs von Balthasar tells a similar story: "During the Nominalist period the universe lost its theophanic radiance—the devout no longer encounter God outside but only within themselves. At the same time, the universe loses its hierarchic gradation and collapses into 'matter' which,

There is, he points out, no bar to "rethinking Biblical religion within the universe" as distinct from the cosmos. For Aristotle and other Greek thinkers, the cosmos was necessarily limited and bounded. This aspect of what he calls the "cosmic imaginary" has been superseded even by religious believers, such as Origen, Nicholas of Cusa, Pascal, and others. There may be other features of the ancient view that can be discarded without losing what is of value.

In this book I have been advocating a return from universe to "cosmos," but not uncritically or without the revision of many features of the ancient view. With this in mind, it is worth noting Taylor's point that the transformation from cosmos to universe is not simply due to "the progress of science," as though empirical science had disproved the hierarchy of being and we had simply moved on, leaving a few pockets of resistance to be mopped up later. The change from sacred cosmos to secular universe was due mainly to ideology and the pressure of social change. Science itself has not disproved God, and religion will never disappear, though it may take new forms.

Taylor's account helps us to understand how the philosophical and theological shift brought about by nominalism and voluntarism could be part of a global transformation that is much more than intellectual, involving many social, psychological, political, economic, and spiritual factors. At the end of it all he leaves us in a series of dilemmas, because he explicitly does not want simply to remove us from the "immanent frame" of modernity—which he describes as a natural or this-worldly order understood in its own terms without reference to the supernatural. On the one hand, he is very far from denying the supernatural as essential "for purposes of ultimate explanation, or spiritual transformation, or final sense-making."[4] On the other, he thinks we cannot "fix the contemporary situation" by applying a philosophical and theological analysis, because "history cannot be separated from the situation it has brought about."[5] Nor can we simply escape our dilemmas by flipping back to an earlier Golden Age. What we need to overcome is the very dualism for which "modernity"

itself without essence, becomes that which is merely mathematically calculable and which is present to be exploited by man" (452).

4. Taylor 2007, 594.

5. Ibid., 776.

and "Christendom" are the stark alternatives. His sympathies lie with hard-to-categorize figures such as Charles Péguy and Gerard Manley Hopkins, for whom

> creative renewal was only possible in action which by its very nature had to have a certain temporal depth. This kind of action had to draw on the forms which had been shaped in the deeper past, but not by a simple mechanical reproduction, as with "habit," rather by a creative re-application of the spirit of the tradition.[6]

Taylor's book puts the challenge very neatly. While we cannot step outside history—and Christianity confirms that view, by redeeming history!—history's forward movements, its great creative leaps, often involve retrievals of insights and ideas from the past (*ressourcement*). What we now need to retrieve is the hierarchy of levels of reality, a sense of the "analogy of being," which allows for an order of divine wisdom (an "ontic Logos," as Taylor puts it) shaping creation. While we cannot anymore accept the details of medieval cosmology, this fundamental intuition of the Logos has never been disproved. In fact, as we have seen, the most recent developments in science could be said to confirm it.

Liberate Your Freedom

Nevertheless, talking in this way is likely to arouse fear for the intellectual gains won in the Enlightenment. If reason is to be "put in its place," as merely a mode of participation in the divine Logos, will this not put theology once more in a position of overconfident superiority? Under the conditions set by secular modernity, it appears that the legitimate autonomy of the intellectual disciplines, especially the human and natural sciences, must inevitably be threatened by any controlling influence from the side of faith—so that, in order to defend academic and intellectual freedom, the Church must not be allowed to influence academic appointments or the curriculum, for example. But the assumptions that underlie this opposition are

6. Ibid., 747.

false.[7] As we have seen, the Liberal Arts were intended to conduce to freedom of mind, and they were developed and nourished by the Catholic Church. But the post-nominalist world has a very strange and dangerous conception of freedom, and this conception distorts the way we think.

The best way to put this might be that the Christian conception of freedom is *larger and fuller* than the modern conception, for it includes both vertical and horizontal dimensions. The horizontal dimension encompasses the world we see directly, and the vertical allows for degrees of being and value, invisible realms, formal causality, and so on. A popular misconception has it that medieval man thought the world was flat, and modern science gave us a round world floating in an infinite space. But the truth is almost the opposite of this. Medieval man inhabited a three-dimensional cosmos which has now been largely replaced by a flat universe, with no ontological depth. It is not a question of size, or even of infinite spaces. An infinite field is still essentially flat. In pure modernity there can be no up or down, no getting closer to hell or heaven, and there are no sacred places and times which participate in the divine. Of course, there are parts of the world that we like better than others, and many that we can enjoy intensely while life lasts, or else places where we fear to go, but these all lie within the horizontal plane of the world, defined as that which our senses reveal and explore.

In the traditional "three-dimensional" world, the self was encouraged to collect itself together in a point, in order to attach itself to a vertical axis, a spiritual "path." The way heavenward always involved the integration of the self by a variety of means, the chief of which was continual prayer or remembrance of God. Conversely, the way to "hell," or eternal frustration, was through the integration of the self around a *rejection* of prayer, or a hatred of it. Modernity, on the other hand, rejects the existence of the vertical altogether, or the very possibility of thinking in terms of up and down. This leads to a world in which the self is fragmented and dissipated. We consume more and more to become less and less; we spread ourselves, as Bilbo

7. For an extended analysis of why they are false, see again Schindler 1996, in the chapter "On Meaning and the Death of God in the Academy."

said to Gandalf, like butter over too much bread. This is a world of pure consumerism.

In a flatter universe, freedom had to be reconceived as entirely a matter of movement within the horizontal plane. I am assumed to be "freer" the more places I can go to, the more things I can choose on the supermarket shelf, the more people I can have relationships with. And that is why the Church claims today to be in the business of *liberating human freedom*, by making known the beauty of truth in its fullness.[8] For she is making known a whole other dimension of human freedom, the "vertical," and the power of Christ to enable us to ascend in that dimension (with our bodies, as Christ himself did), closer to God through virtue, and eventually into the eternal life of God itself. It takes a power from beyond ourselves (i.e., the grace of God) to liberate our will to that extent, since without that help "I do not do what I want, but I do the very thing I hate" (Rom. 7:15). The grace stemming from the sacrifice of Christ frees us to follow him, if we choose to do so.

The Two Wings

Recent Catholic debates about the crisis of belief have come to focus on the relationship of "faith and reason." The separation of the two affects everything: science, economics, art, politics, and education. It lay behind 9/11 and spawned the War on Terror. Debates about contraception and gay marriage are conditioned by it. If faith and reason are indeed incompatible, if they are mutually exclusive, then we are forced to choose between them. Once we have chosen, the energies of human nature will be channeled by our choice and we will shape

8. For example, "Although non-Christians can be saved through the grace which God bestows in 'ways known to him,' the Church cannot fail to recognize that such persons are lacking a tremendous benefit in this world: to know the true face of God and the friendship of Jesus Christ, God-with-us. Indeed 'there is nothing more beautiful than to be surprised by the Gospel, by the encounter with Christ. There is nothing more beautiful than to know him and to speak to others of our friendship with him.' The revelation of the fundamental truths about God, about the human person and the world, is a great good for every human person, while living in darkness without the truths about ultimate questions is an evil and is often at the root of suffering and slavery which can at times be grievous" (Congregation for the Doctrine of the Faith 2007, # 7).

the world accordingly. Either way, it will be a war for supreme power over the world: in our own name, or in God's.

Freedom and knowledge go together. In order to be free, we must *know*. But religious believers know things *both* by reason *and* by faith. These two remain distinct, and it is not a choice between one and the other (as it would be if faith were, as its critics allege, simply believing something without evidence and clinging to it no matter what). Their relationship is one of reciprocal illumination. Faith needs reason to illuminate and unfold its own content; reason needs faith to teach it things it cannot know by its own powers, as well as things it may have forgotten. In his 1998 encyclical *Fides et Ratio* Pope John Paul famously likens them to the two wings of a single bird.[9]

In speaking of "reason," however, as Pope Benedict XVI said in his Regensburg Lecture of 2006, we must "overcome the self-imposed limitation of reason to the empirically verifiable." We are helped in overcoming this limitation by a distinction many ancient authors made between discursive and contemplative intelligence, or between a lower and a higher kind of reason—reason at the level of soul (*ratio* or *dianoia*) and reason at the level of spirit (*intellectus* or *nous*).

> The medievals distinguished between the intellect as *ratio* and the intellect as *intellectus*. *Ratio* is the power of discursive thought, or searching and re-searching, abstracting, refining, and concluding [*cf.* Latin *dis-currere*, "to run to and fro"], whereas *intellectus* refers to the ability of "simply looking" (*simplex intuitus*), to which the truth presents itself as a landscape presents itself to the eye. The spiritual knowing power of the human mind, as the ancients understood it, is really two things in one: *ratio* and *intellectus*: all knowing involved both. The path of discursive reasoning is accompanied and penetrated by the *intellectus*' untiring vision, which is not active but passive, or better, *receptive*—a receptively operating power of the intellect.[10]

This distinction may be correlated with St. Paul's division of the human person into body, soul, and spirit (*soma*/*psyche*/*pneuma*) in

9. "Faith and reason are like two wings on which the human spirit rises to the contemplation of truth" (John Paul II 1998, prolog). Cf. *The Two Wings of Catholic Thought* (Foster and Koterski 2003).

10. Pieper 1998, 11–12.

1 Thessalonians 5:23, and the more ancient division within the human soul between *nefesh*, *ruah*, and *neshamah* (the animal, mental, and spiritual aspect of the soul, according to Jean Borella's interpretation).[11] The Carmelite mystics from St. Teresa of Avila to St. Teresa Benedicta of the Cross (the martyr-philosopher otherwise known as Edith Stein) have also explored this "tripartite" anthropology,[12] and St. Bonaventure's *Itinerarium Mentis in Deum* provides us with a model of the fully developed, three-level human person based on St. Francis's vision of the six-winged seraph.[13] It seems to me that we need such a distinction here if we are truly to make sense of the Pope's argument. In other words, a third dimension has to be introduced into cognition itself, otherwise faith will appear entirely extrinsic to reason. This goes right to the heart of our concern in this book. How do we overcome the dualism of faith and reason? How do we prepare ourselves for flight?

The divorce of faith from reason led to the subordination either of faith to reason (in modernism, positivism, etc.) or of reason to faith (in the various forms of fideism and extreme biblical fundamentalism). But the seeds of the divorce lay in its reduction of reason to discursive thinking alone. Cognition has been afflicted by the same forces that afflict our freedom, and so in order to bring reason and faith together again we must understand both differently, situating them in a richer, deeper, three-dimensional world. We must understand that faith is not blind, but is a light that enables us to see even the natural world more clearly. And we must understand that reason is naturally open

11. Borella 2001 104–9.

12. Henri de Lubac, SJ, advocates an anthropology based on the ternary body-soul-spirit rather than a dualism of body and soul in his article "Tripartite Anthropology" (see Bibliography). Edith Stein's contribution may be found in her *Finite and Eternal Being*, 459–64.

13. Here there are *three* pairs of wings, not just two: sensation and imagination forming the lower pair, faith and reason the middle, and what he terms "intelligence" and "*synderesis*" the higher. Intelligence and *synderesis* are the faculties that enable us to contemplate first Being (the One) and then the Good (God revealed as three Persons). They represent the third "level" of the human person, the spirit, first in its natural perfection and second as imbued with supernatural grace. But even the natural perfection of intellect cannot be attained except by virtue of supernatural faith, through contemplative ascent using the middle pair of wings (as John Paul II indicated).

to God and in need of God. If we close it off to the transcendent, we do violence to its nature.

Faith is not opposed to reason, but it does function as a constant goad, a challenge, a provocation to reason. Faith claims to stand beyond reason, to speak from the place that reason seeks. But it does not claim to *understand* what it knows, and it should not usurp the role of reason in that sense, any more than it should contradict it. The resolution lies not in faith, nor yet in reason, but in love. We are perennially tempted to reduce Christianity to something less than itself: either to power (will, faith, law) or to philosophy (knowledge, reason, wisdom). Nominalists tend to do the former. Realists tend to do the latter. But the solution to this supreme problem in binary logic is through a third and higher thing: love, in which both will and knowledge are reconciled and held in balance—or rather, in which both are transcended. God is love, in which both will and knowledge are comprised.

Whatever your intellectual quarry, if you pursue it to its ultimate lair, you will find the mark of love in the very nature of things. What is magnetism, asks the Victorian poet Coventry Patmore in *The Rod, the Root, and the Flower,* "but the echo of the senseless rock to the very voice of far-off Love, and the effect of the kiss of God transmitted through the hierarchies of heaven and earth to the lips of the least of beings?"

Faith orients reason toward the transcendent, so that reason remains open to a light from above. "The intellect must seek that which it loves: the more it loves, the more it desires to know."[14] But unless we develop some sense of what lies above faith and reason, as well as what lies below, the art of flight will elude us. A disenchanted world is one viewed through the eyes of reason when reason is looking downward. To use the Pope's metaphor, one wing is drooping, no longer reaching for the sky. Even if the wing of faith flaps frantically on the other side, the person will remain earthbound. The things it sees will become opaque and dark, no longer radiant, because they will no longer seem to possess an interior, or any intrinsic relationship to the ideas and the wisdom and the love of God. This is the world

14. John Paul II 1998, # 42.

of darkness and dust that many of us inhabit. But it is as easy and as difficult as it has always been to raise our heads to the sky. The angels are closer than we think.

And the way is open. The intellect seeks truth, and it seeks beauty for truth's sake, but the substance of truth is love.

Bibliography

Al'Arabi, Ibn. 1980. *Ibn Al'Arabi: The Bezels of* Wisdom. Trans. R. W. J. Austin. New York: Paulist Press.

Alexander, Christopher. 2004. *The Phenomenon of Life*. Book 1 of *The Nature of Order: An Essay on the Art of Building and the Nature of the Universe.* Berkeley: Center for Environmental Structure. Available from www.patternlanguage.com.

Balthasar, Hans Urs von. 1968. *Love Alone: The Way of Revelation.* London: Sheed & Ward.

———. 1982. *The Glory of the Lord: A Theological Aesthetics.* Vol. 1, *Seeing the Form.* San Francisco: Ignatius Press.

———. 1991. *The Glory of the Lord: A Theological Aesthetics.* Vol. 5, *The Realm of Metaphysics in the Modern Age.* San Francisco: Ignatius Press.

———. 2000. *Theo-Logic.* Vol. 1, *The Truth of the World.* San Francisco: Ignatius Press.

Barker, Margaret. 2003. *The Great High Priest: The Temple Roots of Christian Liturgy.* London: T&T Clark.

Barr, Stephen M. 2003. *Modern Physics and Ancient Faith.* Notre Dame, IN: University of Notre Dame Press.

Barron, Robert. 2007. *The Priority of Christ: Toward a Postliberal Catholicism.* Grand Rapids, MI: Brazos Press.

Barrow, John D. 2003. *The Constants of Nature: From Alpha to Omega.* London: Vintage.

Begbie, Jeremy. 2008. *Resounding Truth: Christian Wisdom in the World of Music*. London: SPCK.

Benedict XVI, Pope. 2007. "Address to the Participants in the First European Meeting of University Lecturers," Rome, June 23. Online at www.vatican.va.

Birzer, Bradley J. 2007. *Sanctifying the World: The Augustinian Life and Mind of Christopher Dawson*. Front Royal, VA: Christendom Press.

Bloom, Allan. 1987. *The Closing of the American Mind*. New York: Simon & Schuster.

Bohm, David. 1996. *On Creativity*. London: Routledge.

Bolton, Robert. 2005. *Self and Spirit*. Hillsdale, NY: Sophia Perennis.

Bonaventure, St. 1955. *De Reductione Artium ad Theologiam*. Trans. Emma Thérèse Healy. Works of Saint Bonaventure, vol. 1. St. Bonaventure, NY: Franciscan Institute, Saint Bonaventure University.

———. 1956. *Itinerarium Mentis in Deum*. Trans. Philotheus Boehner, OFM. Works of Saint Bonaventure, vol. 2. St. Bonaventure, NY: Franciscan Institute, Saint Bonaventure University.

Borella, Jean. 2001. *The Secret of the Christian Way: A Contemplative Ascent Through the Writings of Jean Borella*. Ed. and trans. G. John Champoux. Albany, NY: State University of New York Press.

Bortoft, Henri. 1996. *The Wholeness of Nature: Goethe's Way of Science*. Hudson, NY: Lindisfarne Press.

Bouyer, Louis. 1988. *Cosmos: The World and the Glory of God*. Petersham, MA: St. Bede's.

———. 1999. *The Invisible Father*. Edinburgh: T&T Clark.

Burckhardt, Titus. 1987. *Mirror of the Intellect: Essays on Traditional Science and Sacred Art*. Cambridge: Quinta Essentia.

———. 1995. *Chartres and the Birth of the Cathedral*. Ipswich: Golgonooza Press.

Burtt, Edwin Arthur. 1932. *The Metaphysical Foundations of Modern Science*. London: Routledge & Kegan Paul.

Caldecott, Stratford. 1998. "A Science of the Real: The Renewal of Christian Cosmology." *Communio* 25:3. Revised at www.secondspring.co.uk/articles/scaldecott11.htm.

———. 2005. *The Power of the Ring: The Spiritual Vision Behind* The Lord of the Rings. New York: Crossroad. [UK edition 2003. *Secret Fire: The Spiritual Vision of J. R. R. Tolkien*. London: DLT.]

———. 2006. *The Seven Sacraments: Entering the Mysteries of God*. New York: Crossroad.

Chadwick, Henry. 1981. *Boethius: The Consolations of Music, Logic, Theology, and Philosophy*. Oxford: Oxford University Press.

Chapp, Larry S. 2006. "*Deus Caritas Est* and the Retrieval of a Christian Cosmology." *Communio* 33:449–72.

Charbonneau-Lassay, Louis. 1991. *The Bestiary of Christ*. Trans. and abr. D. M. Dooling. New York: Parabola Books.

Charles, HRH The Prince of Wales. 1989. *A Vision of Britain: A Personal View of Architecture*. New York: Doubleday.

Chesterton, G. K. 1932. *Chaucer*. London: Faber & Faber.

Coleridge, S. T. 1983. *The Collected Works of Samuel Taylor Coleridge*. Ed. James Engell and W. Jackson Bate. Vol. 1. Bollingen Series LXXV. Princeton, NJ: Princeton University Press.

Congregation for the Doctrine of the Faith. 2007. *Doctrinal Note on Some Aspects of Evangelization*. Vatican City: Libreria Editrice Vaticana.

Critchlow, Keith. 1994. "The Platonic Tradition on the Nature of Proportion." In *Rediscovering Sacred Science*, ed. Christopher Bamford, 133–68. Edinburgh: Floris Books.

Cunningham, Conor. 2002. *Genealogy of Nihilism: Philosophies of Nothing and the Difference of Theology*. London and New York: Routledge.

Daly, Cardinal Cahal B. 2004. *The Minding of Planet Earth*. Dublin: Veritas.

Damascene, Hieromonk. 1999. *Christ the Eternal Tao*. Platina, CA: Saint Herman Press.

Dawson, Christopher. 1952. *Understanding Europe*. London and New York: Sheed & Ward.

———. 1989. *The Crisis of Western Education*. Steubenville, OH: Franciscan University Press.

de Lubac, Henri. 1996. "Tripartite Anthropology." In *Theology in History*, 117–200. San Francisco: Ignatius Press.

Dupré, Louis. 1993. *Passage to Modernity*. New Haven, CT: Yale University Press.

Durandus, Guilielmus. 2007. *The Rationale Divinorum Officiorum: The Foundational Symbolism of the Early Church, Its Structure, Decoration, Sacraments, and Vestments*. Louisville, KY: Fons Vitae.

Durrwell, F.-X. 1990. *The Spirit of the Father and Son: Theological and Ecumenical Perspectives*. Middlegreen: St. Paul Publications.

du Sautoy, Marcus. 2008. *Finding Moonshine: A Mathematician's Journey Through Symmetry*. London: Fourth Estate.

Eliade, Mircea. 1959. *The Sacred and the Profane: The Nature of Religion*. New York: Harcourt, Brace & World.

Florensky, Pavel. 1997. *The Pillar and Ground of the Truth: An Essay in Orthodox Theodicy in Twelve Letters*. Trans. Boris Jakim. Princeton, NJ: Princeton University Press.

Foster, David Ruel, and Joseph W. Koterski, eds. 2003. *The Two Wings of Catholic Thought: Essays on* Fides et Ratio. Washington, DC: Catholic University of America Press.

Friedländer, Paul. 1969. *Plato: An Introduction*. Trans. Hans Meyerhoff. Bollingen Series LIX. Princeton, NJ: Princeton University Press.

Gamble, Richard M., ed. 2007. *The Great Tradition: Classic Readings on What It Means to Be an Educated Human Being*. Wilmington, DE: ISI Books.

Gregorios, Paulos Mar. 1987. *The Human Presence: Ecological Spirituality and the Age of the Spirit*. Amity, NY: Amity House.

Guardini, Romano. 1994. *Letters from Lake Como: Explorations in Technology and the Human Race*. Grand Rapids, MI: Eerdmans.

———. 1998. *The End of the Modern World*. Wilmington, DE: ISI Books.

Guénon, René. 2001a. *The Great Triad*. Ed. Samuel D. Fohr and trans. Henry D. Fohr. Hillsdale, NY: Sophia Perennis.

———. 2001b. *The Reign of Quantity and the Signs of the Times*. Hillsdale, NY: Sophia Perennis.

———. 2001c. *Symbols of Sacred Science*. Ed. Samuel D. Fohr and trans. Henry D. Fohr. Hillsdale, NY: Sophia Perennis.

Hadot, Pierre. 1995. *Philosophy as a Way of Life: Spiritual Exercises from Socrates to Foucault*. Ed. Arnold I. Davidson and trans. Michael Chase. Oxford: Blackwell.

Hallyn, Fernand. 1990. *The Poetic Structure of the World: Copernicus and Kepler*. New York: Zone Books.

Hanby, Michael. 2003. "Creation without Creationism: Toward a Theological Critique of Darwinism." *Communio* 30:4, 654–94.

Hani, Jean. 2007. *The Symbolism of the Christian Temple*. San Rafael, CA: Sophia Perennis.

Hart, David Bentley. 2003. *The Beauty of the Infinite: The Aesthetics of Christian Truth*. Grand Rapids, MI: Eerdmans.

Huerre, Denis, OSB. 1994. *Letters to My Brothers and Sisters: Living by the Rule of St. Benedict*. Collegeville, MN: The Liturgical Press.

Hugh of St. Victor. 1991. *The* Didascalicon *of Hugh of Saint Victor: A Medieval Guide to the Arts*. Trans. Jerome Taylor. New York: Columbia University Press.

Hughes, John. 2007. *The End of Work: Theological Critiques of Capitalism*. Oxford: Blackwell.

Iamblichus. 1988. *The Theology of Arithmetic: On the Mystical, Mathematical and Cosmological Symbolism of the First Ten Numbers*. Trans. Robin Waterfield. Grand Rapids, MI: Phanes Press.

Izutsu, Toshihiko. 1984. *Sufism and Taoism: A Comparative Study of Key Philosophical Concepts*. Berkeley, CA: University of California Press.

John Paul II, Pope. 1985. "The Holy Spirit Proceeds from the Father and the Son." General Audience, November 20. www.vatican.va.

———. 1998. *Fides et Ratio: On the Relationship Between Faith and Reason*. Vatican City: Libreria Editrice Vaticana.

———. 2006. *Man and Woman He Created Them: A Theology of the Body*. Trans. Michael Waldstein. Boston, MA: Pauline.

Joost-Gaugier, Christiane L. 2006. *Measuring Heaven: Pythagoras and His Influence on Thought and Art in Antiquity and the Middle Ages*. Ithaca, NY: Cornell University Press.

Kahn, Charles H. 2001. *Pythagoras and the Pythagoreans: A Brief History*. Indianapolis, IN: Hackett Publishing Company.

Koestler, Arthur. 1989. *The Sleepwalkers: A History of Man's Changing Vision of the Universe*. London: Penguin Books.

Koyré, Alexandre. 1957. *From the Closed World to the Infinite Universe*. Baltimore, MD: Johns Hopkins University Press.

Lang, U. M. 2004. *Turning Towards the Lord: Orientation in Liturgical Prayer*. San Francisco: Ignatius Press.

Lawlor, Robert. 1982. *Sacred Geometry: Philosophy and Practice*. London: Thames & Hudson.

Leclercq, Jean, OSB. 1978. *The Love of Learning and the Desire for God: A Study of Monastic Culture*. London: SPCK.

Lewis, C. S. 1947. *The Abolition of Man, or Reflections on Education with Special Reference to the Teaching of English in the Upper Forms of Schools*. New York: Macmillan.

Lundy, Miranda. 2005. *Sacred Number: The Secret Qualities of Quantities*. Glastonbury: Wooden Books.

MacIntyre, Alasdair. 1990. *Three Rival Versions of Moral Enquiry: Encyclopaedia, Genealogy, and Tradition*. Notre Dame, IN: University of Notre Dame Press.

Mâle, Emile. 1958. *The Gothic Image: Religious Art in France of the Thirteenth Century*. San Francisco: Harper Torchbooks.

Maritain, Jacques. 1954. *Creative Intuition in Art and Poetry*. London: Harvill Press.

Martineau, John. 2006. *A Little Book of Coincidence in the Solar System*. Glastonbury: Wooden Books.

Meerson, M. A. 1998. *The Trinity of Love in Modern Russian Theology.* Quincy, IL: Franciscan Press.

Merrigan, Terence. 1991. *Clear Heads and Holy Hearts: The Religious and Theological Ideal of John Henry Newman.* Louvain: Peeters Press.

Meyer-Baer, Kathi. 1970. *Music of the Spheres and the Dance of Death: Studies in Musical Iconology.* Princeton, NJ: Princeton University Press.

Morgan, Vance G. 2005. *Weaving the World: Simone Weil on Science, Mathematics, and Love.* Notre Dame, IN: University of Notre Dame Press.

Nasr, Seyyed Hossein. 1996. *Religion and the Order of Nature.* Oxford: Oxford University Press.

Naydler, Jeremy, ed. 1996. *Goethe on Science: An Anthology of Goethe's Scientific Writings.* Edinburgh: Floris Books.

Newman, John Henry, Cardinal. 1982. *The Idea of a University.* Ed. Martin J. Svaglic. Notre Dame, IN: University of Notre Dame Press.

———. 2001. *The Works of Cardinal John Henry Newman*, vol. 3. Notre Dame, IN: University of Notre Dame Press. The essay referred to is "The Mission of St. Benedict," written in 1958.

O'Collins, Gerald. 1999. *The Tripersonal God: Understanding and Interpreting the Trinity.* London and New York: Continuum.

Olsen, Glenn W. 2006. "The Return of Purpose." *Communio* 33:666–81.

Peterson, Erik. 1964. *The Angels and the Liturgy.* New York: Herder & Herder.

Philo. 1981. *Philo of Alexandria: The Contemplative Life, the Giants, and Selections.* Trans. David Winstone. New York: Paulist Press.

Pickover, Clifford A. 2005. *A Passion for Mathematics: Numbers, Puzzles, Madness, Religion, and the Quest for Reality.* Hoboken, NJ: John Wiley.

Pickstock, Catherine. 1998. *After Writing: On the Liturgical Consummation of Philosophy.* Oxford: Blackwell Publishers.

Pico della Mirandola. 1965. *On the Dignity of Man, On Being and the One, Heptaplus.* Trans. Charles Glenn Wallis, Paul J. W. Miller, Douglas Carmichael. Indianapolis: Bobbs-Merrill.

Pieper, Josef. 1998. *Leisure the Basis of Culture.* Trans. Gerald Malsbary. South Bend, IN: St. Augustine's Press.

Plato. 1892. *The Dialogues of Plato Translated into English.* Trans. Benjamin Jowett. 3rd ed. Oxford: Clarendon Press. Available online from http://oll.libertyfund.org.

Polanyi, Michael. 1964. *Personal Knowledge: Towards a Post-Critical Philosophy.* San Francisco: Harper & Row.

Ratzinger, Joseph, Cardinal. 1995a. *"In the Beginning . . .": A Catholic Understanding of the Story of Creation and the Fall*. Grand Rapids, MI: Eerdmans.

———. 1995b. *The Nature and Mission of Theology: Approaches to Understanding Its Role in the Light of Present Controversy*. San Francisco: Ignatius Press.

———. 1996. *A New Song for the Lord*. New York: Crossroad.

———. 2000. *The Spirit of the Liturgy*. San Francisco: Ignatius Press.

Reale, Giovanni. 1997. *Towards a New Interpretation of Plato*. Ed. and trans. John R. Catan and Richard Davies. Washington, DC: Catholic University of America Press.

Reid, Constance. 2006. *From Zero to Infinity: What Makes Numbers Interesting*. 50th anniversary ed. Wellesley, MA: A. K. Peters.

Rose, Michael S. 2001. *Ugly as Sin*. Manchester, NH: Sophia Institute Press.

Ruhr, Mario von der. 2006. *Simone Weil: An Apprenticeship in Attention*. London: Continuum.

Sayers, Dorothy L. 1973. *A Matter of Eternity: Selections from the Writings of Dorothy L. Sayers*. Ed Rosamond Kent Sprague. London & Oxford: Mowbray.

Schindler, D. C. 2004. *Hans Urs von Balthasar and the Dramatic Structure of Truth: A Philosophical Investigation*. New York: Fordham University Press.

———. 2006. "Christian Imagination: The Reformation of Causality and the Iconoclasm of the Spirit." *Communio* 33:4, 521–39.

Schindler, David L. 1996. *Heart of the World, Center of the Church: Communio Ecclesiology, Liberalism, and Liberation*. Grand Rapids, MI: Eerdmans.

Schloeder, Steven J. 1998. *Architecture in Communion*. San Francisco: Ignatius Press. See also www.liturgicalenvirons.com.

Schmitz, Kenneth L. 2005. *The Recovery of Wonder: The New Freedom and the Asceticism of Power*. Montreal: McGill-Queen's University Press.

Schneider, Michael S. 1994. *A Beginner's Guide to Constructing the Universe: The Mathematical Archetypes of Nature, Art, and Science*. New York: HarperCollins.

———. 2006. *Constructing the Cosmological Circle*. Constructing the Universe Activity Books, vol. 5. From www.constructingtheuniverse.com.

Scola, Angelo, Cardinal. 2007. "The Primordial Relationship between God and the Human Person in Catholicism and Islam." Washington, DC: Intercultural Forum for Studies in Faith and Culture, Pope John Paul II Cultural Center. Online at www.cisro.org.

Stein, Edith. 2002. *Finite and Eternal Being: An Attempt at an Ascent to the Meaning of Being*. Trans. Kurt F. Reinhardt. Washington, DC: ICS Publications.

Stewart, Ian. 1996. "A Day in the Life of a Year." *New Scientist*, January 6.

Sutton, Daud. 2005. *Platonic and Archimedean Solids*. Glastonbury: Wooden Books.

Taub, Liba Chaia. 1993. *Ptolemy's Universe: The Natural Philosophical and Ethical Foundations of Ptolemy's Astronomy*. Chicago: Open Court.

Tavener, John. 1999. *The Music of Silence: A Composer's Testament*. Ed. Brian Keeble. London and New York: Faber & Faber.

Taylor, Charles. 1989. *Sources of the Self: The Making of the Modern Identity*. Cambridge University Press.

———. 2007. *A Secular Age*. Cambridge, MA: Harvard University Press.

Taylor, James S. 1998. *Poetic Knowledge: The Recovery of Education*. State University of New York Press.

Ward, Maisie. 1949. *Gilbert Keith Chesterton*. London: Sheed & Ward.

Ward, Michael. 2008. *Planet Narnia: The Seven Heavens in the Imagination of C. S. Lewis*. Oxford: Oxford University Press.

Weil, Simone. 1956. *The Notebooks of Simone Weil*, vols. 1 and 2. London: Routledge & Kegan Paul.

———. 1957. *Intimations of Christianity Among the Ancient Greeks*. London: Routledge & Kegan Paul.

———. 1968. *On Science, Necessity, and the Love of God*. London: Oxford University Press.

———. 1973. "Forms of the Implicit Love of God." In *Waiting for God*. San Francisco: Harper & Row.

Wittkower, Rudolf. 1998. *Architectural Principles in the Age of Humanism*. New York: St. Martin's Press.

Wölfflin, Heinrich. 1984. *Renaissance and Baroque*. London: Collins.

Readers who have enjoyed this book will find further reading and useful links at www.secondspring.co.uk/books.

Index